Warman's® DOLLS

Antique to Modern

Mark F. Moran

Identification and Price Guide

©2004 KP Books

Published by

kp books
An imprint of F+W Publications, Inc.

**700 East State Street • Iola, WI 54990-0001
715-445-2214 • 888-457-2873**

Our toll-free number to place an order or obtain
a free catalog is (800) 258-0929.

Library of Congress Catalog Number: 2004093903

ISBN: 0-87349-654-X

Designed by Jamie Griffin

Edited by Dennis Thornton

Printed in United States of America

Dedication

This book is dedicated to Arline Hunziker and Joan Hunziker Dean, whose generosity in sharing their love of dolls helped to make this guide a reality.

Words of Thanks

This gathering of information for this book was greatly assisted by the resources and good wishes of the following:

Georgia Rankin's "Collector Showcase" of Sturgeon Bay, Wis.

James D. Julia Inc. Auctioneers and Appraisers of Fairfield, Maine. (See page 256)

Dawn Herlocher, author of Antique Trader's Doll Makers and Marks and 200 Years of Dolls, 2nd Edition.

Graves Doll Studio of Rochester, Minn. (See page 242)

"Antie Clare's" Doll Hospital & Shop of North St. Paul, Minn. (See page 245)

Contents

The Play's The Thing

Arline Hunziker and her daughter, Joan Hunziker Dean, holding their favorite dolls: Arline's is a J.D. Kestner bisque head from about 1890, and Joan's is an Armand Marseilles Scottish boy, from the same era.

Joan Dean has a clear memory of the first doll that made an impression on her. It belonged to her mother, Arline Hunziker.

"It was an old doll that was always kept in a trunk," Joan, 51, recalled. "It was never displayed, just tucked away in that trunk."

Like forbidden fruit, the aura of the doll in the trunk enticed her. Though it was out of reach, "It was very special to me, and I knew I was not to play with that."

That E.I. Horsman celluloid doll ("like a Dream Baby," Arline says)—new in 1924 when it arrived at Christmas—was just the first of dozens of dolls the mother and daughter of Rochester, Minn., would acquire over the years. But it wasn't until the late 1960s that the pair discovered doll collecting could be a shared experience.

"That didn't start until we went to an antique show held at the YMCA in Mankato (Minn.) in 1969," said Arline, 85. Joan spotted a Floradora doll by Armand Marseilles (active 1885 to 1930s, Marseille was one of the largest suppliers of bisque doll heads in the world). The doll had a new wig and repainted body, and a red dress.

"I think it was that dress that really attracted her," Arline said with a laugh. "She wanted that doll so bad, and I thought, "Oh, Joan, that's ridiculous, it was $45!"

Arline admits, "I kept dragging my feet," because it was so expensive in 1960s dollars. But Joan was not to be denied.

"We went home, and over supper discussed the doll, and I remember I had $150 in my savings account," Joan said, finally deciding, "I think that I should buy this doll."

"I was touched by it," Joan said, "so we went back to the show and bought it."

After they began attending doll shows, their collecting senses became sharper. And Joan discovered she was attracted to china-head dolls, especially the "pet names," those with their names written in script on the front of the shoulder plate.

"Her name is Bertha," said Joan, pointing to the largest of a group of china heads sitting like little busts on a shelf in her home, and now surrounded by her larger sisters and brothers made of bisque, composition, and vinyl that she and her mother have collected for the last 35 years.

Bertha was a head only (as they were originally sold beginning in the 1840s) and at the time Joan felt the doll was incomplete without a body. She made a new body for Bertha, with replacement limbs from Mark Farmer of California, a well-known 1960s retailer that sold doll parts and kits by mail order. Farmer catalogs featured parts to complete various china-head dolls, including Jennie June and Godey Lady Dolls, plus original designs and character dolls, including vinyl Kewpies, American Indian rag dolls, Hummel dolls, and folk dolls from various countries; doll furniture, toy cast-iron "Crescent" and "Queen" stoves, and sets of dollhouse miniatures.

"I insisted on getting some dolls that mom didn't like, figuring that I could talk her into it," Joan said. "I was probably more drawn to china heads, while Mom was more attracted to the bisque dolly faces.

"I liked the idea then—and I still do today—that these were dolls that were played with," Joan said, picking up a small china head with worn and fading blonde hair.

"It looks like some little girl was sucking on this one," Joan added. "That played-with look is still important."

Arline and Joan also started going to the library to consult doll books, including Dorothy Coleman's reference books from the 1970s, which have propelled many a collector in the hunt for dolls.

"We spent evenings poring over (the books)," Joan recalled. "But though we liked the look (of the vintage bisque-head dolls), we always looked at the price first."

The longer they collected, the more they came to realize that many of the 19th century doll makers were interconnected, either through bodies, heads, or modes of dress.

"Mom kind of went in her own direction with some interests," Joan said, "that I learned to appreciate over time, like ethnic dolls.

"I remember that, as a girl, I had just one Barbie. Maybe another girl in the neighborhood would have a few Barbies, if she was an only child, but usually you only had the one.

Shoulder Head
19" metal shoulder head, unmarked, blue stationary glass eyes, open mouth, blonde wig, leather body, bisque hands, wearing a cotton dress, pink socks and shoes; all original, near mint, seldom found in this condition.

$250+

"Mom always picked out dolls that had brown hair, because I had brown hair. I never got a blonde doll, unless it only came with blonde hair. My dad made a wardrobe for my Terri Lee doll clothes, and my mom would make the outfits."

Joining a doll club was also essential for their collecting lives. The more they learned, the more they wanted to know, and there was always another door to open to get more information.

Fellow enthusiasts introduced them to the United Federation of Doll Collectors. And they shared discoveries with friends who traveled to Europe "to pick out the best Bru dolls they could find," dolls that could sell for tens of thousands of dollars today. Being able to learn from a quality collection helped sharpen their eyes as well. Sometimes the camaraderie of doll collectors was a revelation.

"Here is the trust level that my mother gained," Joan said, still with a little awe in her voice.

Arline spotted a nice Kestner doll at an antique show in 1973—it was $50. But Arline wanted to get the opinion of some dealer friends who were at a show in Minneapolis. So she asked the seller if she could take it to her friends, get their thoughts, and on her way home either return the doll or buy it.

Déposé E9J
19" Déposé E9J doll. Blue paperweight eyes and fine bisque on a straight-wrist, eight-ball-jointed Jumeau (unmarked) body. Wearing antique shoes, a pale green dress, large bow on the back and a pale green bonnet. Original spring in head. Minor wear and paint loss at body joints.

$9,000-$10,000

"This was a lady in her 80s," Arline said, "and I didn't know her personally, only saw her at a few antique shows."

The woman let Arline take the doll—no deposit, no guarantees, only her word.

"I left her and thought, 'This is awful, even asking her if I could take the doll as a favor like this.'"

She bought the doll.

Joan's father, Eugene, also got interested.

"He was a door-to-door salesman of siding and roofing, so he was able to get into people's attics as part of his work, and he came home with quite a few dolls, especially composition and hard plastic," Joan said. "One time he came home with a decaying rubber doll (probably made of Magic Skin) and he thought he was doing us a real favor."

Today, after seeing what a talented doll restorer can do with the hard-plastic head of a Magic Skin doll, Arline and Joan don't turn up their noses at mid-20th century dolls anymore.

There have been missteps along the way, but they were learning experiences.

"Once my husband came home with a doll in its original box," Arline recalled, "and I think I used it later as a shipping box. Now, I checked it first to see if there was any name on it, and there wasn't, just the ties to hold the doll inside. But I remember thinking at the time, 'What am I going to do with this box?'"

They learned some important tips from veteran doll sellers.

One woman had drawers full of Jumeau dolls that she would store face down, "and every once in a while if I wanted a real thrill, I would go look at those beautiful French dolls, knowing that they were FOUR-HUNDRED DOLLARS!!" Joan said. (Now, of course, a seller could easily add a zero to that price.)

"Dolls with sleep eyes have to be stored face down," Arline said, "because if those eyes fall back in, either the eyes or the head could be damaged (they are easily scratched from rolling around inside the head), and then they have to be reset."

And at some time, they realized how important it was have to have the right style clothing on the right doll.

"That's where mom's sewing skills came in handy," Joan said. "We would buy old fabric, or she would have old cloth stored away in a trunk" (that same trunk that held the "forbidden" doll). Drawing on her "stash" of fabric, most of Arline's costumes were designed "out of her head."

As their understanding of doll heads and body construction grew, the pair got more particular when shopping for a new acquisition.

23" Parian shoulder head, blonde molded hair, cloth body, bisque hands and feet, wearing a gold velvet dress.

$100+

"We wouldn't buy a doll if it seemed a bit odd, or if it had a cracked head," Joan said. "Today, I would buy a damaged doll if the price is right, but back then, they had to be perfect."

Joan remembers a special doll that she received for her 17th birthday: a pen-wiper doll, all bisque, with a long two-section gown lined with cotton used for wiping pen points. Made to be hung on a wall or near a desk, it had a dual purpose, like the "half dolls" whose bodies may also serve as tops for pincushions or brush handles.

"And I was not impressed (with the pen-wiper doll), so I returned it," Joan said, now holding it in her hands. She took it back to the seller and exchanged it for a Parian doll—"this one in the striped dress," Joan said, pointing to a small figure in the corner of an oak china cabinet.

"Later, I went back, saw that (the pen-wiper doll) was still there, and bought it back, realizing what it was."

That's when she knew she had a collecting life.

"In old dolls, you accept a certain amount of imperfection, because of the hand-painting, and the way they're made," Joan said as she picked up a bisque-head baby doll that seemed to be having an allergic reaction. The right eyehole was slightly smaller than the left, giving one side of the face a puffier look.

"That's an example of a basic imperfection in what I think is a very fine doll," Joan said.

Joan then picked up a vintage Dream Baby and held it next to a modern reproduction of a slightly smaller baby doll. The modeling of the Dream Baby's face—soft, lustrous, and warm—was a stark contrast to the angular, mannequin-like face of the modern doll.

"It's only been in the last five years or so that I've purchased repro dolls, because after you've been collecting for a while, you can spot a repro just like that," Joan said. "It's just a feeling that you get after a while."

Arline and Joan are not attracted to so-called "artist dolls."

"They're statues," Joan said, meant to sit on a shelf and show off the artist's skill, "but not to be played with."

Each doll in the mother-daughter collection bears a large string tag with detailed records about when the doll was purchased, the price, who it was bought from and where, and the doll's dimensions and characteristics, including clothing. All that information is also kept separately in a notebook.

"Record-keeping is important for study and reference," Arline said, "and for giving presentations."

Their advice for beginning collectors?

"Buy what you like and buy the best quality you can find," Joan said.

What about the next generation? Joan has bought dolls for her two daughters—Bridget and Paula—to enjoy, not as treasures, "but to play with."

And when those dolls need new clothes?

"Mom ("Grandma" now) is still sewing outfits from fabric out of that old trunk."

How to Use This Book

Warman's Dolls: Vintage to Modern is organized by the material used to make dolls, rather than by maker or era. This allows collectors to quickly focus their search for information, since dolls are often categorized by the material used to make the head. There are separate sections on dolls made of cloth, composition, metal, papier-mâché and wax, porcelain (including bisque, china, and Parian), synthetic materials (celluloid, hard plastic, latex, rubber, and vinyl), and wood.

Each of those sections is then organized alphabetically by maker or style, and each maker or style contains an alphabetical breakdown by doll names (including details about marks and construction techniques), and then by size, from smallest to largest.

There are also sections on artist dolls, automatons, clothing and accessories, a bibliography, dollhouses, doll repair and restoration, doll clubs, a glossary of doll collecting terms, and a few words on reproductions.

Artist Dolls

Though some collectors think of them as simply pretty statues, others consider artist dolls to be a logical extension of the doll maker's art. Many of the artists are members of either the National Institute of American Doll Artists (NIADA) or Original Doll Artists Council of America (ODACA). Material, workmanship, subject matter, and visual or decorative appeal are all part of their collectibility.

For more information on makers belonging to these two organizations, visit their Web sites at www.niada.org and www.odaca.org.

Kathy Redmond
Two Kathy Redmond heads. First, elderly lady; second, French dame with elaborate hairdo, fancy full hat and numerous ribbons on rear of head. Overall fine.

$250-$300/pair

St. Nicholas
24" Lewis Sorensen wax St. Nicholas. Holding accessories in his hands and a Christmas tree on his back. Blue inset glass eyes with a well-defined and detailed face. Very good original condition.

$1,400-$1,600

Martha Thompson Lady
Martha Thompson lady head (Martha Thompson, born Huntsville, Ala., 1903, died 1964). With molded bust, black hat worn to side with large white feather plumes. Blonde hair with braids rolling down side of head, partially covering ear, and floral adornments. All original and in excellent condition.

$250-$300

Princess Margaret Rose
Martha Thompson "Princess Margaret Rose" head (Martha Thompson, born Huntsville, Ala., 1903, died 1964). Brown curled hair adorned with gold tiara encrusted with jewels. Head is marked on rear of shoulder plate. All original and in excellent condition.

$185-$225

Martha Thompson Lady
12" Martha Thompson lady (Martha Thompson, born Huntsville, Ala., 1903, died 1964). Excellent condition but dress is extremely shredded, some damage to flowers on top of head.

$300-$400

Betsy
14" Martha Thompson "Betsy" (Martha Thompson, born Huntsville, Ala., 1903, died 1964). Signed on back of shoulder plate. On a body with original clothing. Excellent condition.

$300-$400

Martha Thompson Lady
18" Martha Thompson lady (Martha Thompson, born Huntsville, Ala., 1903, died 1964). Multiple black curls swept to face, wearing a tiered lace dress adorned with silk roses. All original and in excellent condition.

$150-$200

Queen Victoria
18" Martha Thompson young "Queen Victoria" (Martha Thompson, born Huntsville, Ala., 1903, died 1964). Wearing a cream-colored outfit with train, braided hair in front of exposed ears and wraps around to rear bun, with a gold crown encircling bun. All original and in excellent condition.

$350-$400

Princess Margaret Rose
19" Martha Thompson "Princess Margaret Rose" (Martha Thompson, born Huntsville, Ala., 1903, died 1964). Wearing a parachute silk gown with a gold and pearl tiara (small repair to tiara).

$450-$550

Jenny Lind
20" Martha Thompson "Jenny Lind" (Martha Thompson, born Huntsville, Ala., 1903, died 1964). Glass inset eyes, bun in rear of head and coils on the sides. Hair is highlighted with porcelain roses. Wearing a tiered gown. All original and in excellent condition.

$350-$450

Princess Carlotta
20" Martha Thompson "Princess Carlotta" (Martha Thompson, born Huntsville, Ala., 1903, died 1964). On a marked cloth body, exposed ears, curls dropping down onto shoulder plate, which has a molded pearl necklace. Wearing a crown with encrusted jewels and a gold hair net. All original and in excellent condition.

$600-$700

Queen Elizabeth II

21" Martha Thompson "Queen Elizabeth II" (Martha Thompson, born Huntsville, Ala., 1903, died 1964). With curls to rear and exposed ears, wearing a tiara with encrusted jewels. Molded necklace, and cream-colored lace dress. All original and in excellent condition.

$500-$600

Lady and Gentleman

Two Martha Thompson dolls, lady and gentleman (Martha Thompson, born Huntsville, Ala., 1903, died 1964). Gentleman is all original and in excellent condition; lady is in excellent condition, but missing dress.

$300-$400/pair

George and Martha Washington

Two Martha Thompson dolls, dressed as George and Martha Washington (Martha Thompson, born Huntsville, Ala., 1903, died 1964). All original and in excellent condition.

$750-$850/pair

Alice in Wonderland

"Alice in Wonderland" set by Eunice Tuttle. Jointed all-bisque artist dolls with a parlor background. Includes Alice, Tweedle-Dee and Tweedle-Dum, the Mad Hatter, the Queen of Hearts, and the Walrus and the Carpenter. In a Plexiglas cube. Feet have been re-glued to Tweedle-Dee and Tweedle-Dum. It appears that Alice had something in her right hand that is now missing.

$900-$1,000/set

Angel Baby
2 1/4" angel baby by Eunice Tuttle. Jointed all-bisque artist doll of an angel baby lying on a baby quilt with pillow, and contained in a Plexiglas cube. Fine condition.

$150-$200

Prince Edward
3 1/2" Prince Edward by Eunice Tuttle. Jointed all-bisque artist doll of Prince Edward holding a scepter with palatial background, and contained in a Plexiglas cube. Fine condition.

$275-$325

Marguerita
3 3/4" infant Marguerita by Eunice Tuttle. Jointed all-bisque artist doll of baby Marguerita, in its original box. Fine condition.

$250-$300

Stroller
4" girl with doll and stroller by Eunice Tuttle. Jointed all-bisque artist doll of a girl with a stroller and doll with the background of a house, contained in a Plexiglas cube. Fine condition.

$350-$400

Renoir Girl
4" Renoir girl by Eunice Tuttle. Jointed all-bisque artist doll of a girl in a navy dress holding a watering can in one hand and daisies in the other. Fine condition.

$300-$400

Girl
4" girl by Eunice Tuttle. Jointed all-bisque artist doll of a girl in a yellow dress with blue crochet bonnet. Fine condition.

$150-$200

Girl
4" girl by Eunice Tuttle. Jointed all-bisque artist doll of a girl in a yellow dress with matching hair ribbon with open mouth and teeth. Fine condition.

$175-$225

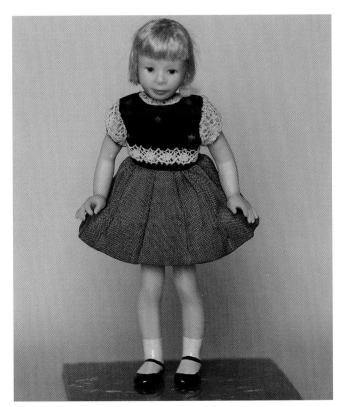

Girl
4" girl by Eunice Tuttle. Jointed all-bisque artist doll of a girl in a green party frock. Fine condition.

$150-$200

Girl with Wagon
4" girl with wagon by Eunice Tuttle. Jointed all-bisque artist doll of a girl pulling her wagon. Fine condition.

$150-$200

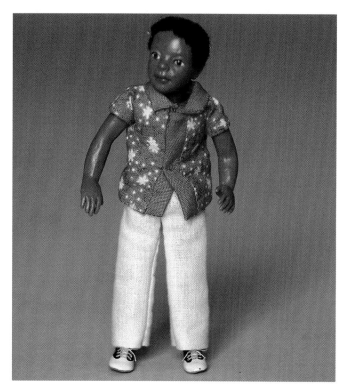

Chet
4" black boy "Chet" by Eunice Tuttle. Jointed all-bisque artist doll of a young black boy in his original box (his outfit matches another Tuttle doll, "Candy"). Fine condition.

$200-$250

Candy
4" black girl "Candy" by Eunice Tuttle. Jointed all-bisque artist doll of a young black girl in her original box (her outfit matches another Tuttle doll, "Chet"). Fine condition.

$200-$250

Bride and Groom
4 1/4" bride and groom by Eunice Tuttle. Jointed all-bisque artist dolls of a bride ond groom, contained in a Plexiglas cube. Bride is missing her lower right leg and her pinkie is broken.

$100-$125/pair

Girl with Hoop
4 1/2" jointed bisque girl with hoop by Eunice Tuttle. Jointed all-bisque artist doll of a girl holding her hoop in an outside winter scene, contained in a Plexiglas cube. Fine condition.

$300-$400

Girl
4 1/2" jointed girl with doll by Eunice Tuttle. Jointed all-bisque artist doll of a girl holding her doll and standing in front of a table, contained in a Plexiglas cube. Fine condition.

$400-$450

Mary Ellen Cassatt
4 1/2" Mary Ellen Cassatt by Eunice Tuttle. Jointed all-bisque artist doll seated on a chair, and contained in a Plexiglas cube. Fine condition.

$150-$200

Miss Hatch
4 1/2" Miss Hatch with Baby by Eunice Tuttle. Jointed all-bisque artist doll of a young lady seated in a chair and holding a baby in her lap next to a table with the backdrop of a parlor, and a pony and cart toy on the floor. In a Plexiglas cube. Fine condition.

$300-$400

Automatons

Often intended for the amusement of adults rather than children, the term "automaton" covers a range of mechanical figures, some small enough to sit on a parlor table, others large enough to pull a wagon.

An American popular tabloid during the Civil War told tales of "The Steam Man of the Prairies." "Boilerplate" was a mechanical man developed by Professor Archibald Campion during the 1880s and unveiled at the 1893 World's Columbian Exposition in Chicago. In the late 1890s, inventor Louis Philip Perew constructed an electrically operated mechanical man that was about 7 feet tall.

While some automatons date to the mid-18th century, the golden era of these figures large and small was from about 1860 to 1910.

Made around the world, mechanical dolls are evaluated based on costuming, condition, visual appeal, and intricacy of movement. Generally, value increases in direct relation to the doll's complexity. The more intricate the movements and the greater their number, the more valuable the automata. Working condition is important, since repairs can be costly.

Well-known manufacturers of automatons—usually operated by spring-driven works—include Rousselot, Phalibois, Vichy, Fleischmann and Blodel, Lambert, and Roulette de Camp. Marks may be found on keys or on the inside of the housings. Doll heads were supplied by various doll manufacturers and were marked accordingly.

Animated dolls were first introduced in Germany and share some similarities with automatons. The spring clockwork of the automata is replaced by a rotating mechanism; turning a crank causes the figure to move, usually in a stiff and awkward style. Generally, the value of

these is determined more by charm and visual appeal than from the complexity of their movements.

Autoperipatetikos employ a clockwork mechanism within a walking body. Most are about 10" tall and may have patent marks.

Cymbalers contain a pressure-activated bellows mechanism within their bodies. When compressed, the arms come together. Heads are usually made of bisque and commonly resemble a baby or clown.

Walking, kicking, crying, and talking dolls were known as Gigoteur. First patented in 1855 by Jules Steiner, the body houses a flywheel regulator and clockwork mechanism. They are typically marked "1," "2," "3," or unmarked.

Marottes from France and Germany fall somewhere between a doll and a toy. They incorporate music boxes and often have whirling figures. Frequently Marottes are made of papier-mâché and decorated to represent a variety of characters from clowns to animals.

Swimming dolls, also known as Ondines, were once advertised as "Parisian Mechanician for Adult Amusement." They were made with either a bisque or celluloid head and a cork body, with jointed wooden arms and legs that simulated swimming when wound by a key.

Early walking and talking dolls are often found with chain mechanisms. Others have wire arrangements connecting the arms and feet, a technique first used by Schoenhut wooden dolls. The talking device in early talking dolls consists of a bellows in the body that was activated by pulling strings, exerting pressure, or moving some part of the body. Some collectors also include phonograph dolls in this category.

Girl with Mirror
French Lambert automaton of girl with mirror and powder puff (9" by 12 1/2" by 18"). A closed-mouth Tete Jumeau #5 with blue paperweight eyes and bisque lower arms standing at a dressing table with mirror. When activated, the doll turns her head from left to right, occasionally lowering her head and powdering her nose. She then turns to the left to glimpse at herself in the mirror held in her left hand. Clothing (probably not original) in fragile condition. Some trim missing from base. Two tunes play when activated. (Pierre Francois Jumeau, Paris, founded about 1842.)

$4,000-$5,000

Schoolboy and Fifi O'Toole
French schoolboy and Fifi O'Toole automatons manufactured by Roulette de Camp, each 12" tall. Boy with schoolbag and a young girl holding an infant. When wound, they sway from left to right while also turning their heads. In very fine all original condition, boy's mechanism is sticky, probably in need of light lubrication.

$1,200-$1,500/pair

Mozart
French automaton "Mozart" (8 1/2" by 10" by 12"). Paper label attached to bottom, "Serenade de Schubert" and "Menuet de Mozart." Automaton has drawer that, when pulled open, activates the mechanism. The bisque-head pianist proceeds to move his hands across the keys while raising and lowering his head and turning side to side. Pin attached to drawer that activates mechanism is missing. This is just a minor repair and should not detract from the value.

$3,500-$4,000

Tete Jumeau
Tete Jumeau automaton (6" by 6" by 16"). An open-mouth Tete Jumeau #2 with brown paperweight eyes. When activated, the girl raises her right hand to smell her flowers while her head nods and left arm moves. Clothing and wig are older replacements, rub to end of nose. Various movements are inoperative. (Pierre Francois Jumeau, Paris, founded about 1842.)

$1,200-$1,500

Lady with Egg
French automaton of a lady with egg, 16" tall, base 4" by 4 1/2". When activated, she taps the egg with a cymbal and the top of the egg opens, revealing a glass-eyed monkey peeking out. The head has blue paperweight eyes and is made of bisque with a closed mouth, and marked "M1" on rear. Clothing is made of silk and, if not original, shows some age. Overall very fine and in working condition.

$4,500-$5,500

Automatons

Punch

Jumeau automaton "Punch"-type figure with cymbals, 19" tall, base 5" square. Brown-eyed Tete Jumeau #4 automaton in original costume and wig, clapping her cymbals together while nodding her head from left to right. Costume is frail with significant fraying. Base has been re-covered in maroon velvet. Overall movements and music are fine. (Pierre Francois Jumeau, Paris, founded about 1842.)

$4,500-$5,500

Smoking

French Jumeau smoking automaton, 23" tall, base 6" square. When activated, music plays, the gentleman nods his head and also swivels from left to right while raising his right hand, which contains an ivory-type cigarette holder, to take a puff of his cigarette. Marked Tete Jumeau #2 on head with blue paperweight eyes and open mouth with original wig, hat, pants, and shoes (coat has been replaced). Overall very good condition.

$6,000-$7,000

Cloth Dolls

Many of the dolls featured in this section were later mass-produced, after being created in the home by makers responding to families, friends, or just creative urges.

Unlike the bisque works of famous European makers, many of the cloth dolls here are the creations of American innovators. These include Julia Jones Beecher, Albert Brückner, Martha Chase, Xavier Roberts, Louise R. Kampes, Marysia "Mollye" Goldman, Johnny Gruelle, Gertrude Rollinson, Ella Smith, and Izannah Walker.

Also included here are the two widely emulated European makers, Lenci and Steiff.

Cloth Doll Makers

Effanbee Doll Co., founded circa 1910 (Klumpe)

Effanbee is an acronym for Fleischaker & Baum, New York. The company imported and distributed cloth display or souvenir dolls made in Spain by Klumpe. (Also see composition, synthetic.)

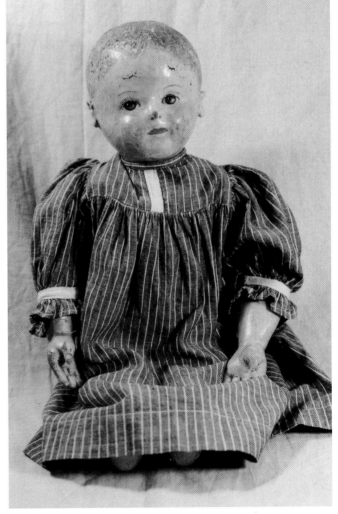

Baby
This Martha Chase baby is 16" long and weighted with sand. The ears and thumbs are stitched on, and the head also has a stitched pattern like that found on a softball. It shows the facial wear typical of these dolls. Depending on condition, prices range upwards from

$500

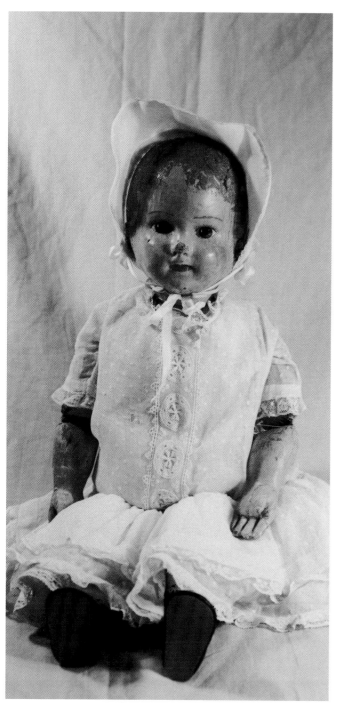

Birdwatcher
12" Klumpe "Birdwatcher."

$80+

Hospital Doll
This Martha Chase "Hospital Doll" is 21" long. Some came with holes in the nostrils and ears for use in hospital training classes on the care of infants. It shows the facial wear typical of these dolls. Depending on condition, prices range upwards from

$500

Mae West
12" Klumpe (Mae West?), felt stuffed body, painted face, blonde hair, white cotton dress.

$70+

Golfer and Dancer
Two Klumpe dolls, Golfer and French dancer, taller 12".
$70+ each

Spanish Dancer
12" Klumpe Spanish Dancer holding baby.

$80+

Architect
12" Klumpe Architect.

$80+

Folk Art Dolls

The term "folk art" is really one of perspective. The pieces that we now value as folk art often were not considered works of art by their makers. Rather, they had a form and function that were determined by the necessities of their day, or by the emotional investment in their creation. This is especially true of vintage folk art dolls.

When trying to determine the value of a folk doll, remember that folk art comes from a tradition outside of academic circles, and includes items both whimsical and utilitarian, whether elaborate or starkly simple. There are vast differences in the quality of folk dolls, depending on the talent and skill of the maker. Many are one-of-a-kind examples, and this makes general pricing difficult. The inventiveness and charm of a given doll can be more crucial factors than condition.

Topsy-turvy

This folk art "topsy-turvy" doll (two half dolls joined at the waist, one black and one white) dates to the late 1860s and comes with a homemade blanket. It has hand-painted features and measures about 12" long. Depending on size, appeal, and condition, such dolls may cost anywhere from $150 to $450. Dolls with a family history or detailed provenance—or attributed to a known maker—may bring much more.

$150-$450

Käthe Kruse, founded 1910

Based in Bavaria since the mid-1940s, vintage Käthe Kruse Dolls were made of waterproof treated muslin, cotton, wool, and stockinet. The earliest dolls were marked in black, red, or purple ink on the bottom of the foot with the name "Käthe Kruse" and a three- to five-digit number. Celluloid dolls were also made in the late 1930s, and hard plastic in the early 1950s.

Adults

Käthe Kruse adult figures, set of three. Two women, one bearded man. Some touchup to facial features of man, which has some flaking to paint. Overall soiling, water staining to man's costume and to the stockinet legs of the women.

$5,500-$6,500/set

Lenci, founded 1919

Established in Turin, Italy, Lenci felt dolls are the standard against which all similar dolls are measured. They were first created by Elena Konig Scavini, and her brother, Bubine Konig.

According to company records, the Lenci trademark was registered in 1919 as a child's spinning top with the words "Ludus Est Nobis Constanter Industria" (taken from the Latin motto, freely translated to mean "To Play Is Our Constant Work"), forming the acronym "LENCI."

Lenci was the first company to produce dolls using the pressed-felt method to give the faces dimensional character.

Lenci Dolls are often referred to in series, such as "Mascotte" for the small 9" characters; "Hard Faced" for composition, mask, or flocked plastic heads; and "Bambino" for bent-limb babies. Code numbers are also commonly used; for example, children with hollow, felt torsos are in the 300 series, pouty-face dolls in the 1500 series, ladies or gentlemen in the 165 series, and girl dolls in the 700 series.

Lenci dolls may be marked with a hangtag, clothing label, or a purple or black "Lenci" stamp on the bottom of a foot. This stamp has a tendency to wear off.

Floppy Limb Felt Dolls: all felt; swivel neck; long arms and legs; mohair wig; felt disk eyes sewn to face; painted cheeks; felt lips; original, felt costume; typically marked with hang tag attached to clothing.

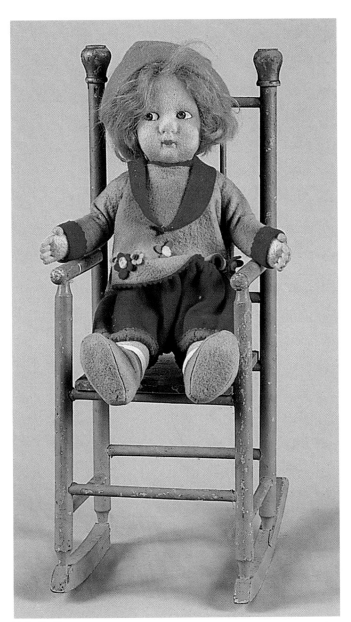

Felt Doll
11" old Lenci felt doll, moveable limbs, well played with.

$125+

Felt Doll
11" old Lenci felt doll, painted face, moveable limbs, significant wear.

$75+

Italian Felt
12" Italian felt Lenci. Souvenir of the 1991 Exposition of Dolls Regional Conference. Excellent condition and retains hangtag on front.

$180-$220

Matador
14" Italian felt Lenci matador. All-original Lenci character with brown painted eyes. Some light soiling and fading of cheek color.

$450-$550

Italian Felt
19" Italian felt Lenci. Blonde mohair wig, brown side-glancing eyes, and original wool costume. Overall fading, paint on lips has been touched up, some holes to right hand. Shoes and socks are replaced.

$250-$350

Boy and Girl
Pair of 20" Lenci dolls. Boy with sandy blonde mohair wig, overall soiling, repairs to body, dressed in black wool pants. Girl with curly blonde mohair wig, overall soiling and fading, replaced felt dress and hat, some wear to legs.

$450-$550/pair

Girl

22" Lenci girl, felt stuffed body with jointed limbs, painted side-glancing eyes, all felt outfit with dress, coat, leggings and shoes, curly blonde hair; all original and mint.

$1,000+

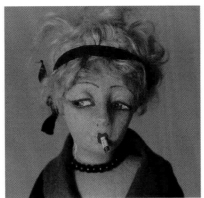

The Smoker

25" Italian felt Lenci flapper doll known as "The Smoker." Character with original clothing and mohair wig. Some moth holes to side of face and neck, overall dusting with some fading.

$600-$700

Boudoir Jester

28" Lenci boudoir jester doll, felt painted face, cloth body, white satin jester outfit with black felt dots, black satin hat and black felt shoes; all original and mint.

$1,500+

Lenci-Type Dolls

Companies that produced copies of Lenci dolls include: Alma, Alpha, Alexander, American Stuffed Novelty, Amfelt, Averill, Chad Valley, Celia, Davis, Deans, Eros, Fiori, Giotti, La Rosa, Magis, Perotti, Pori, Raynal, and Wellings.

While many such dolls do not have the same appeal as Lenci, the all-felt dolls made by R. John Wright, winner of the "Jumeau Award" in the category of Outstanding International Doll Artist, are an exception. His contemporary creations are acknowledged to be of the highest quality.

Lenci-Type Dolls

Four 15" Lenci-type dolls, possibly Pori, all original, felt stuffed, jointed limbs, painted side-glancing eyes, each wearing clothing made of felt and organdy; all original.

$800+ each

Pillow and Rag Doll Makers

Pillow or rag dolls were printed or lithographed, designed to be cut, sewn, and stuffed at home. Detailed instructions were printed alongside the figures. Many early printed dolls were produced in New England, the center of American textile manufacturing in the 1880s, and it was at this time that patented rag dolls appeared in great quantities in the United States.

Care must be taken when purchasing a printed cloth doll. Craft shows offer hundreds of artificially "aged" dolls. Some even have an "attic odor." Intended as accent pieces, they look authentic. One widely circulated copy is the reprint of Palmer Cox Brownies. These convincing reprints even have the original 1892 copyright date. A clue to spotting the reprints is their washed out or faded appearance. They also measure 7" tall. The original Brownies measured 8" and were brightly colored.

Ravca Dolls, established 1930s

Created by Bernard Ravca, originally of Paris. Ravca won first prize at the Paris Fair with his two life-sized figures of a Normandy peasant and his wife. Ravca came to the U.S. during World War II and became an American citizen in 1947.

French Couple
18" Ravca silk sculptured man and woman, marked "Made in France," painted character faces, cloth bodies, sculptured hands, he carries a fish basket and she carries knitting, each with leather shoes.
$250-$300 each

Sheppard & Co., "Philadelphia Baby", circa 1900

Also know as the Sheppard Baby, these life-size cloth dolls were sold at the J.B. Sheppard Linen Store on Chestnut Street in Philadelphia. The designer, maker, and exact dates of manufacture are unknown.

Philadelphia Baby
20" Philadelphia Baby with trunk and wardrobe. About six outfits, several pairs of shoes, four hats, and many undergarments/pajamas. Wear to face and head, old over-painting to doll. Clothing in very good original condition.
$5,000-$6,000/set

Steiff, founded circa 1880s

Margarete Steiff (1847-1909) was an accomplished seamstress, making women's and children's clothing out of wool felt. In 1880, she designed and created a small felt elephant pincushion. The creature's popularity prompted her to begin commercially producing small, stuffed animals.

According to the Steiff Co., Margarete's nephew, Richard, designed a small, jointed, mohair bear that was exhibited at the 1903 Leipzig Toy Fair.

By coincidence, at about this same time, President Theodore Roosevelt traveled to Mississippi on a hunting expedition. One evening, a bear cub wandered into camp. Roosevelt refused to kill the young bear; instead he chased it back to its mother. The Washington Post's political cartoonist, Clifford Berryman, a member of the hunting party, drew a cartoon of the president chasing the bear. Thereafter, "Teddy's Bear" was in every cartoon Berryman did of Roosevelt. In 1906, at his daughter's wedding reception held at the White House, decorations were Steiff bears dressed as hunters and fishermen. In the next year, one million Steiff bears sold.

The Steiff factory operated for many years as a cottage industry. Women would pick up the raw materials at the factory and return with a finished toy.

Steiff markings have changed several times. In 1892, a camel was used, but never registered. In 1898, the elephant with his trunk forming the letter "S" was used, but again without being registered. The Teddy Bear, introduced as "Petz," was never registered, and competing firms were able to manufacture "Teddy Bears."

An application by Steiff dated December of 1904 seeks a register "for a button in the ear for toys of felt and similar material." Margarete wrote to her customers to inform them: "...From November 1, 1904 on, each of my products, without exception, shall have as my trademark a small nickel button in the left ear."

Steiff also produced dolls advertised as "jovial lads and buxom maidens." They came with felt pressed heads with a seam down the middle of the face, mohair wigs, glass eyes, and large feet.

The features on authentic Steiff dolls are often hand painted and embroidered, and seams are frequently hand sewn, qualities missing from copies.

Hedgehog Family
5" and 7" Steiff Hedgehog family, characters Mom (Micki) and Pop (Mecki), brother, (Macki), and sister, (Mucki); all marked, all original.

$150+/set

Bears
From left: 8" Steiff Zotti bear; 3 1/2" Steiff tiny tan bear; 10" Steiff dog hand puppet.
Zotti, $100; Tiny, $70; Dog, $80

Animals

Four Steiff animals, from left: 5" beaver, 7" monkey (Jocko), 5" lamb (Snucky), 9" monkey, which shakes its head when tail is moved.

Beaver, $65; Jocko, $100+; Lamb, $50; Monkey, $150+

Hedgehogs

Two 10" Steiff Hedgehogs, characters Mom (Micki) and Pop (Mecki), felt stuffed bodies, bur hair, faces are made of a rubberized molded material, all original clothing made of felt and cotton.

$600-$800 each

Marionette
11" Steiff Marionette girl, felt stuff body, painted rubber-like face, yarn hair, felt dress.

$30-$50

Farmer and Lucky
Left, 13" Steiff character Farmer with spade, felt body with fur hair and whiskers, pictured with his friend, Lucky; both have rubber-like molded faces, felt clothing and leather shoes, and original tags.

Farmer, $90+; Lucky, $65

Farmer and Wife
18" Steiff Farmer (#9112/45) and Farmer's Wife (#9110/43), stuffed felt with ear buttons, painted faces, felt and cotton clothes, leather shoes, all original.

$175+ each

W.P.A. Dolls, 1930s

Made in the United States during the 1930s as part of Franklin D. Roosevelt's New Deal, the Works Progress Administration provided work for artists and seamstresses struggling during the Great Depression. Cloth dolls were created representing characters from fairy tales and folklore, and historical figures from both the United States and various foreign countries.

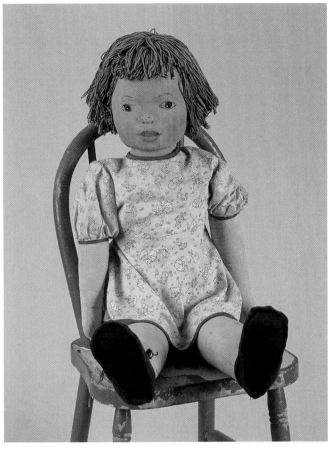

W.P.A.
22 1/2" W.P.A. doll made in Milwaukee, string hair, cloth body rigidly stuffed. This doll was photographed by the Milwaukee Journal.
$1,000+

Izannah Walker, mid-19th century

Izannah Walker of Central Falls, R.I., made dolls with heavily oil-painted features on slightly sculptured faces.

In June of 1873, Walker applied for a patent for her "Rag Dolls." According to patent law, it was illegal for her to have made her dolls for more than two years prior to her application date. There are reports, however, that Walker was making and selling dolls as early as the 1840s.

The patent application described layering and pressing cloth treated with glue in a heated two-part mold. The body was then sewn, stuffed, and glued around a wooden armature. Hands and feet were hand sewn. The entire doll was then hand painted in oil colors. The hair was painted with corkscrew curls or short, straight hair. Other characteristics include applied molded ears, stitched fingers, and either bare feet with stitched toes or painted-on high-laced shoes.

An Izannah Walker doll in very good condition is incredibly rare.

Izannah Walker
18" cloth Izannah Walker doll. Painted ringlets in front of ears and going around head. Brown painted eyes. Dressed in brown floral cotton with red wool slip and muslin underwear. Red cotton poke bonnet, and comes with early patchwork quilt. Normal wear on face and neck with more wear to back of head. Nose has been repaired, and hands and arms are repainted. Much wear to her lower legs and feet with repairs to the ankles, tips of the toes are open exposing horsehair stuffing.
$6,000-$7,000

Other Cloth Dolls

4" hedgehog musicians (Peter Max?) wearing red stocking caps.

$85+/set

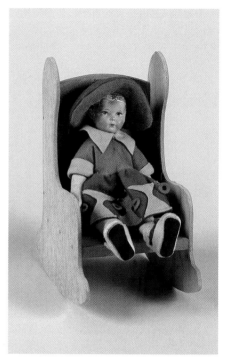

9" cloth over mask face (similar to Nora Wellings), painted eyes, all original felt clothing and shoes.

$70+

From left: 9" silk mask face, cloth body, all original, wool embroidered.

$150-$200

6 1/2" silk mask face, tagged "Capri Treasures of Florence, Italy," all original.

$150-$200

6 1/2" silk mask face, made in Italy, hair braided on sides around ears, all original.

$150-$200

6 1/2" silk mask face, marked "Florence, Italy," cloth body, arms are plastic or celluloid, hair is braided in a bun in back, all original.

$150-$200

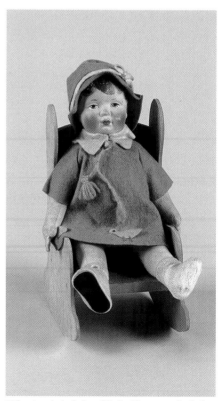

10" painted cloth face (Kathe Kruse-type), cloth hard-stuffed jointed body, wearing original felt green outfit and felt shoes.

$150-$200

Composition Dolls

Often called "compo" by collectors, composition is a generic term to describe a type of doll, popular in the first half of the 20th century, made with molded materials, usually wood-based products. The earliest composition was made from flour, rags, bones, hides, and other waste materials, which were boiled and molded. Later composition was a pulp-based mixture of sawdust and glue, or combinations of plaster.

Some composition heads were coated with a layer of wax. However, because wax and composition expand and contract at different rates, the wax often cracked, producing a crazed surface.

Composition is susceptible to damage caused by environmental extremes. Heat, dampness, and temperature changes quickly take their toll. In general, collectors accept slight crazing as a matter of course for composition dolls. If badly crazed, cracked, peeling, or repainted, values can be reduced considerably.

Composition dolls were made by countless manufacturers in various countries, and many are unmarked.

Various German manufacturers made "Patent Washable Dolls" at the end of the 19th century. Unfortunately, these papier-mâché composition dolls did not live up to their name, and are seldom found in good condition.

Composition Doll Makers

Alexander Doll Co., founded 1923

A true American success story, the company was established by the Alexander sisters — Beatrice Alexander Behman, Rose Alexander Schrecking, Florence Alexander Rapport, and Jean Alexander Disick. Their parents, Russian immigrants Maurice and Hannah Alexander, owned and operated the first doll hospital in the United States.

The first Alexander dolls were made of cloth and had flat faces. Molded faces with painted features quickly followed. In 1929, a line of dolls appeared in trade catalogs advertised as "Madame Alexander." The following year, the Alexander sisters expanded this line, now commonly known as "Madame Alexander Dolls." (Also see cloth, synthetic.)

Madame Alexander Dolls come in more than 6,500 different costumed personalities, so it's important to have the original costume and/or wrist tag to properly identify the dolls.

In 1995 the company was acquired by The Kalzen Breakthrough Partnership, a private capital fund.

Little Genius
22" Madame Alexander character baby, ("Little Genius" or "McGuffey"?), marked "Alexander" on head, composition head and limbs, cloth body, brown hair and sleep eyes, wearing a pink and white dress.

$275-$325

Storybook
Two 7" composition Madame Alexander storybook dolls, painted eyes to the side, painted shoes and socks, blonde mohair wigs, original dresses, one marked "Am. Girl, Madame Alexander, NY, USA" and the other marked "Fairy Princess, Madame Alexander."
$250+ each

Wendy
11" composition doll, marked "Madame Alexander," Wendy face, painted eyes and mouth, blonde wig, wearing an "Alice in Wonderland" outfit.
$100-$150

Pinky
15" Madame Alexander "Pinky," composition head and limbs, sleep eyes, molded hair, cloth body, wearing original net-type dress and bonnet.
$250-$300

Madame Alexander
17" composition, marked "Madame Alexander," jointed body, blue sleep eyes, open mouth with teeth, brown human-hair wig, wearing a white organdy dress.

$600+

Madame Alexander
23" composition baby, marked "Madame Alexander," blue sleep eyes, closed mouth, cloth body and composition limbs, wearing a pink and white sweater dress and bonnet.

$200-$225

Madame Alexander also made an extensive line of personality dolls, and marionettes.

Dionne Quints
Set of 7 1/2" Dionne Quint babies, all marked "Dionne" on heads and "Madame Alexander" on backs, all composition jointed bodies, wearing respective colors (Yvonne, pink; Annette, yellow; Cecile, green; Emelie, lavender; Marie, blue), all original.

$1,300+/set

Dionne Quint

11 1/2" Madame Alexander Dionne Quint doll, marked on head, brown sleep eyes, all composition toddler body, brown hair, wearing original pink organdy dress.

$300+

Dionne Quints

Set of 16" Madame Alexander Dionne Quintuplets, marked on heads, "Madame Alexander Dionne," molded hair, brown sleep eyes, composition heads, shoulder plates and limbs on cloth bodies, in identical white dresses, three missing bibs.

$2,000+/set

Dionne Quint

17" Madame Alexander Dionne Quint doll, head marked "Dionne Alexander," back marked "Alexander," brown sleep eyes, closed mouth, all composition jointed toddler body, wearing pink organdy dress and bonnet with tag marked, "Genuine Dionne Quintuplet Dolls, Madame Alexander."

$600+

Dionne Quint

9 1/2" Madame Alexander Dionne Quint toddler doll, marked "Dionne, Alexander" on head and back, all composition jointed body, human-hair wig over plain head, open mouth, sleep eyes, wearing original pink dress and bonnet.

$800+

Sonja Henie
15" Sonja Henie by Madame Alexander, marked "Madame Alexander Sonja Henie" on head, all composition, open mouth with teeth, redressed in black skating attire and skates.

$450-$500

Sonja Henie
18" Sonja Henie by Madame Alexander, all composition, brown sleep eyes, open mouth with teeth, blonde wig, redressed in aqua taffeta, white marabou, skates.

$550+

American Character Doll Co., 1919 to 1968

Located in New York, 16 styles of composition dolls were made with the trade name Aceedeecee ("ACDC" for American Character Doll Co.).

The first dolls marketed by American Character were composition bent-limb babies with cloth bodies. By 1923, the trade name "Petite" was adopted. In 1928, two years after moving to Brooklyn, American Character received exclusive permission from the Campbell Soup Co. to make Campbell Kids. (Also see synthetic.)

Character Babies: Petite Babies and Mama Dolls; composition head; cloth body; bent limbs; molded and painted hair or good wig; sleep eyes; open or closed mouth; appropriately dressed; typically marked "Petite American Character," "Amer. Char. Doll Co.," "AC," or "Wonder Baby."

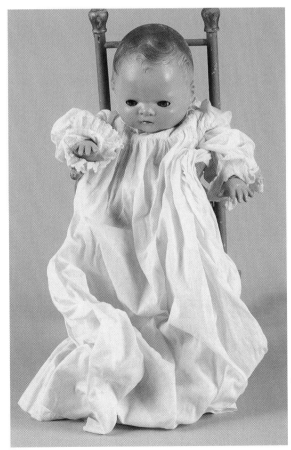

American Character
15" American Character baby, composition head and limbs, blue sleep eyes, cloth body, molded hair, wearing a long white ruffled dress.

$150-$225

Arranbee Doll Co., 1922 to 1959

Founded in New York, the company imported dolls, heads, and parts, and later manufactured its own doll heads. Vogue Doll Co. acquired Arranbee in 1959 but continued to use the "R&B" mark until 1961. (Also see bisque, synthetic.)

Nancy
17" composition R&B Nancy. All-original composition girl with brown sleep eyes, wearing floor-length dress and bonnet. Excellent original condition.

$300-$350

Arrow Novelty Co., founded 1920

Based in New York, Arrow is best known for its Skookum Indian Dolls, designed by Mary McAboy of Missoula, Mt., and patented in 1914. Early doll heads were made of dried apples. Indian blankets were wrapped around wooden frames, leaving very little of the bodies to be seen. The dolls' costumes were made to represent various tribes, with sizes ranging from a few inches to several feet. Most are marked with a paper label on the foot that reads "Skookum Bully Good Indian."

Skookums
15" Skookum Squaw and Papoose, two 11" Squaws, 13" Skookum Chief; mask faces with wigs, wool blankets, wood dowel feet and legs.
$125-$200 each

Berwick Doll Co., 1918 to 1925 (Famlee)

This short-lived firm made the "Famlee" line of composition dolls, patented by David Wiener. They came boxed in a set that included a basic doll body, costumes and several interchangeable heads.

Famlee
Famlee doll with 14 different heads. Circa 1920s. With 14 out of 16 possible heads, and comes with original paperwork and two outfits. Flaking to composition heads.

$350-$400/set

George Borgfeldt & Co., 1881 to late 1950s

This New York importer had exclusive North American rights to distribute the dolls made by firms like Buschow & Beck, Handwerck, Kämmer & Reinhardt, Kathe Kruse, Kestner, and Steiff. American-made dolls distributed by Borgfeldt also included Aetna Doll Co., Bergfeld & Son, Cameo Doll Co., Dreamland Doll, and K&K Toy. Borgfeldt may be best remembered for promoting two dolls that have become icons of doll collecting: Grace Putnam's Bye-Lo Baby and Rose O'Neill's Kewpie. (Also see bisque.)

Many composition dolls were distributed by George Borgfeldt, both German and American made. Examples include: Mamma's Angel Child, Hollikid, Com-A-Long, Daisy, Fly-Lo, and Baby Bo-Kaye. Most have cloth bodies.

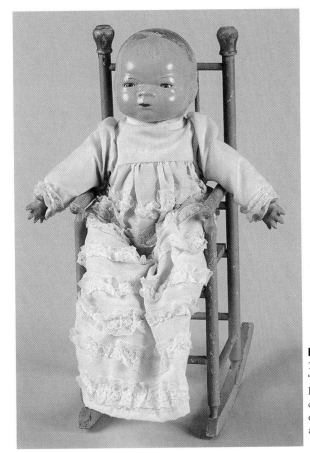

Bye-Lo
12" composition, marked "Grace Storey Putnam Bye-Lo" on head, cloth body, celluloid hands, blue sleep eyes, wearing white cotton and lace dress.

$400-$500

Cameo Doll Co., 1922 to 1970

Located in Port Allegheny, Pa., founder and president Joseph Kallus gained recognition through his work with Rose O'Neill in the modeling of dolls she created, especially the Kewpies. Cameo Doll Co. became the sole manufacturer of composition Kewpies in the United States. George Borgfeldt & Co. distributed them along with other dolls by Cameo such as Bye-Lo, Baby Bo-Kaye, and Little Annie Rooney.

Many Cameo Dolls are considered to be among the finest quality American dolls made in the 20th century. (Also see synthetic.)

It is common for early Cameo Dolls to be unmarked, or to have only a wrist tag. Later dolls were usually well marked and, after 1970, "S71" was added. In 1970, Cameo was acquired by the Strombecker Corp. of Chicago.

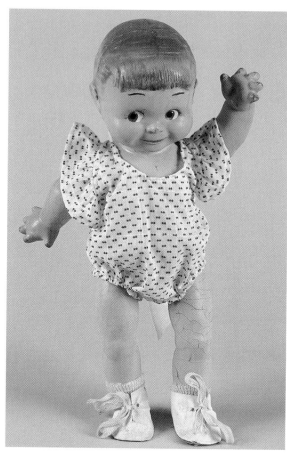

Giggles
14" composition Giggles by Cameo, molded hair with bangs and bun in back (which has a hole through which to pull a ribbon), side-glancing eyes, Kewpie-style mouth, wearing a romper.

$250-$400

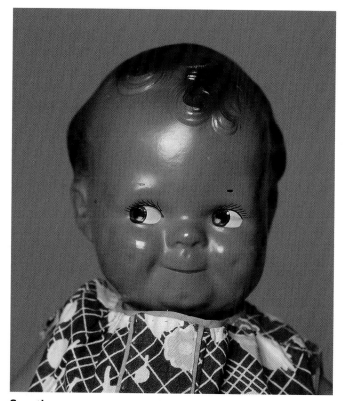

Scootles
13" black composition Scootles. Excellent condition in old clothes and replaced shoes. There is some peeling of paint on neck in back.

$400-$500

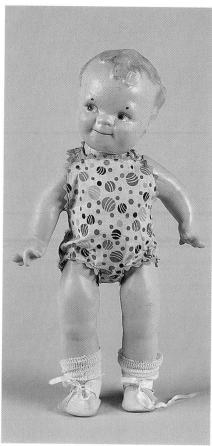

Scootles
16" composition Scootles by Cameo, painted eyes and molded hair, wearing a print romper; some crazing. If perfect,

$500+

Kewpies

From left: 14" composition Kewpie made by Cameo, painted eyes, wearing blue romper.

$300+

4 1/2" bisque Kewpie made by Cameo, with blue wings, wearing pink outfit.

$150+

8" new vinyl Kewpie in red-striped outfit.

$25+

4 1/2" bisque Kewpie, labeled "Rose O'Neill," painted eyes, wearing a long red ribbon.

$150+

Kewpie

11 1/2" composition Kewpie, jointed at shoulders, eyes painted to side, with heart label "Kewpie by Rose O'Neill," molded hair, painted mouth, wearing a red-dotted dress.

$300+

Effanbee Doll Co., founded circa 1910

Effanbee is an acronym for Fleischaker & Baum, New York. The firm's Patsy doll was the first realistically proportioned American-made doll designed to resemble a real child. She was also the first doll for which companion dolls were created, and the first to have a wardrobe and fan club. In 1934, Effanbee introduced "Dydee," the first drink-and-wet doll. The company also imported and distributed cloth display or souvenir dolls made in Spain by Klumpe. (Also see cloth, synthetic.)

American Children: composition body; human hair wig; detailed painted eyes; closed mouth; original, well-made outfit; typically marked "Effanbee/ American Children" or "Effanbee/ Ann Shirley." **Note:** Designed by Dewees Cochra, 1892-1991.

Susan Stormalong

11" Susan Stormalong by DeWees Cochran. With strawberry blonde hair and freckles, with the "SS" mark. Original excellent condition. Human hair lashes are coming loose.

$900-$1,300

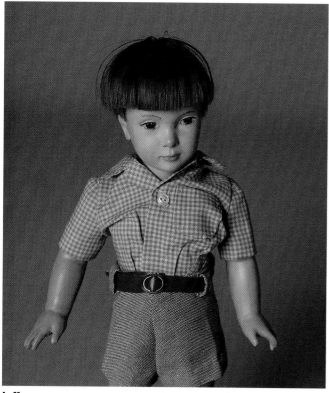

Jeff
12" "Jeff" by Dewees Cochran. Painted blue eyes. Signed "Dewees Cochran" on head. Excellent and all original, some darkening of finish to body.
$1,000-$1,400

Girl
12 1/2" girl by Dewees Cochran. Long golden brown hair. Missing her clothing, her body has some unevenness to finish, small damage at neck socket, and her fingers have been repaired.
$150-$200

Belinda
14" Belinda by Dewees Cochran. Character child signed "BB53 #2." Some unevenness to body finish.
$600-$700

Cindy
14 1/2" Cindy by Dewees Cochran. Character girl with blonde human hair wig. Thumb has split at joint.
$900-$1,100

Angela
15" Angela by Dewees Cochran. Character with blonde human hair, molded smiling open mouth with teeth, and painted blue eyes with lashes. Signed "58" on back of neck. Excellent and all original.

$1,500-$1,700

Angela
15" Angela by Dewees Cochran. Depiction of an older child with molded open/close mouth showing teeth. Dressed in knit sweater and jeans. Signed "AA54 #10." Excellent original condition with light soiling to clothing.
$1,000-$1,400

Susan Stormalong
15" Susan Stormalong by Dewees Cochran. Strawberry blonde hair braided and pulled to the back, wearing a red and green plaid dress. Signed "SS54 #8." Excellent original condition.

$900-$1,300

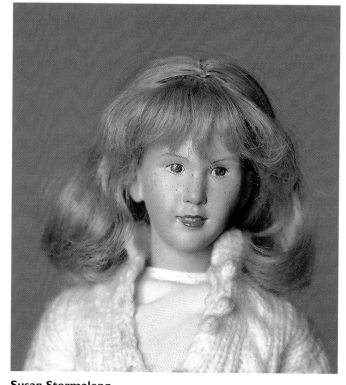

Peter Ponsett
16" Peter Ponsett by Dewees Cochran. Dressed in gray wool jacket and shorts. Signed "PP55 #10." Excellent original condition, with one light scuff on upper lip and one small scuff on chin.

$900-$1,300

Susan Stormalong
16" Susan Stormalong by Dewees Cochran. Character doll, with strawberry blonde hair and painted freckles. Signed "SS55 #10." Some light soiling to clothes.

$750-$850

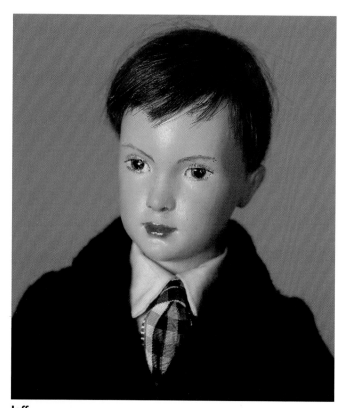

Jeff
16 1/2" Jeff by Dewees Cochran. Signed "JJ55 #10." Wearing blue wool jacket and shorts. Slight unevenness on side of nose and small scuff at brow.

$900-$1,300

Belinda
18" Belinda by Dewees Cochran. Signed "BB58 #9." Original excellent condition.

$400-$500

Boy and Girl

Left, 17 1/2" girl, marked "Effanbee Dewee Design," painted blue eyes, closed mouth, composition body marked "Effanbee USA," wearing red coat and hat.

$1,000+

Right, 18" boy, marked "Effanbee Dewee Design," blond hair, painted eyes, closed mouth, wearing a tweed suit and cap.

$1,000+

Amish Family

11" and 7" Amish couple and child by Effanbee ("Baby Grumpy" molds), composition limbs, cloth bodies, mohair wigs, all original clothing in felt and cotton.

$175 each; $400+/set

Sweetie Pie and Patsy

Left, 19" composition head and limbs Sweetie Pie, flirty blue sleep eyes, brown hair, cloth body, wearing white dress and sunbonnet (possibly original).

$175-$225.

Right, 14" composition Patsy doll, brown sleep eyes, dark blonde wig, wearing a lavender cotton dress and hat.

$125-$200

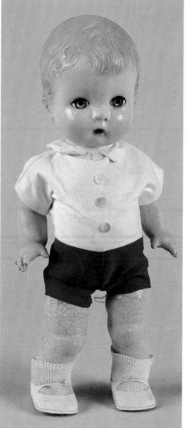

Candy Kid

14" composition Effanbee Candy Kid, molded hair, blue sleep eyes, wearing red shorts and white shirt.

$300+

Head and Hands

16" Effanbee composition head and hands, 1940s, painted eyes, string hair, cloth body.

$75-$125

Little Lady
17 1/2" composition head, marked "Effanbee, Little Lady," composition body, blue sleep eyes, closed mouth, dark hair, wearing original red, white, and blue outfit.

$275+

Ann Shirley
21 1/2" composition, marked "Ann Shirley," brown sleep eyes, reddish brown hair, wearing pink dress and shoes; all original.

$400+

Ann Shirley
27" composition Ann Shirley, brown hair, blue sleep eyes, white blouse and black jumper, brown strap shoes; all original.

$500+

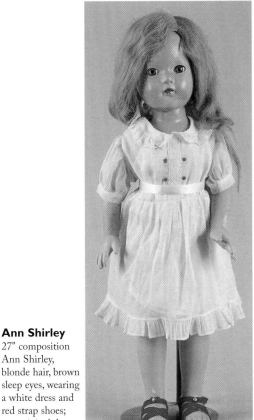

Ann Shirley
27" composition Ann Shirley, blonde hair, brown sleep eyes, wearing a white dress and red strap shoes; not original dress.

$500+

Baby Tinyettes and Patsy
From left: 7" composition baby, marked "Effanbee Baby Tinyette," blue painted eyes, molded hair, wearing white knit outfit.

$180+

11" composition marked "Effanbee Patsy Baby," blue sleep eyes, molded hair, painted mouth, probably original blue coat and hat.

$180-$225

7 1/2" composition toddler, marked "Baby Tinyette," painted brown eyes, painted mouth, wearing blue dress, coat, and hat.

$80-$125

Patsy Baby

Left, 9" composition, marked "Patsy Baby," karakul wig, blue sleep eyes, closed mouth, wearing pink dress and bonnet (possibly original).

$100-$200.

Right, 9 1/2" composition, marked "Effanbee," molded hair, cloth body, painted mouth, blue sleep eyes, wearing pink dress and bonnet.

$60-$90

Patsy

Left, 9 1/2" composition Patsy, molded and painted hair and eyes, jointed, wearing original dress and shoes.

$90-$125

Right, 6" composition Patsy Wee Wetsy, molded hair, painted eyes, jointed, painted socks and shoes, dress not original, otherwise mint.

$200+

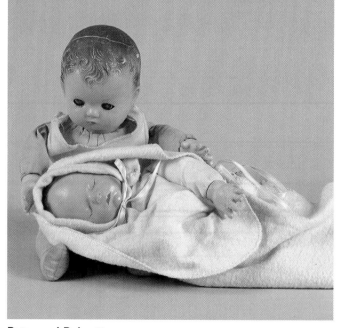

Patsy and Patricia

From left: 11" unmarked Patsy, brown painted eyes, molded hair, painted closed mouth, wearing organdy dress and hat; all original.

$150+

11" composition Patricia Kin, blue sleep eyes, painted mouth, brown hair, wearing blue and white dress (possibly original).

$250-$300

13" composition, marked "Patsy PAT. PEND. DOLL," molded hair, painted brown eyes, redressed in dark teal coat.

$150+

Patsy and Babyette

Seated: 12" composition head, marked "Effanbee Patsy baby" cloth body, composition hands.

$75-$125.

Laying: 11" composition head, marked "Babyette," with painted sleeping eyes, closed mouth, composition hands, cloth body, wearing pink layette.

$75-$125

Patricia
14 1/2" composition, marked "Patricia," brown sleep eyes, painted closed mouth, wearing gold-colored coat and hat; probably not original.
$250-$350

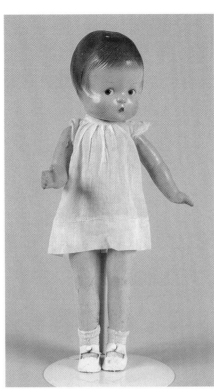

Patsy
14 1/2" composition head Patsy, blue painted eyes to the side, reddish molded hair, composition body.
$100+

Patsy and Jr.
Left, 16" composition doll marked "Effanbee Patsy," green sleep eyes, molded hair, composition body, redressed in coat and hat; doll mint.
$300+

Right, 11" composition, marked "Effanbee Patsy Jr.," molded hair, composition body, redressed in green coat and hat.
$275+

Patsy Ann
19" composition, marked "Patsy Ann," green sleep eyes, molded hair, wearing a checked romper and sunbonnet; all original.
$300+

Patsy Lou
22" composition, marked "Patsy Lou," reddish molded hair, green sleep eyes, wearing a pink wool coat and hat; all original.
$400+

Patsy Lou
22" composition, marked "Patsy Lou," brown sleep eyes, molded hair under wig, wearing a blue sailor dress; all original.
$400+

Patsy Lou

22" composition, marked "Patsy Lou," brown human hair, brown sleep eyes, jointed body, wearing pink dress, shoes and socks.

$375+

E.I. Horsman & Co., founded 1865

Edward Imeson Horsman founded this well-known maker in New York. Beginning in the early 1900s, Horsman produced a variety of popular composition dolls. The dolls had painted hair or wigs, forward- or side-glancing, painted or sleep eyes, open or closed mouths, with or without teeth. As time went on, even more variations were incorporated. Often, a doll was manufactured with a mix of characteristics, entirely different from the norm, or the same mold was given more than one name.

Around 1890, a Russian inventor, Solomon D. Hoffmann, brought his formula for "unbreakable" composition doll heads to America. Horsman eventually was able to secure the rights to Hoffmann's formula.

Horsman is famous for marketing the Billiken doll, originally created by Florence Pretz of Kansas City, Mo. It is reported that during the first six months of production, Horsman sold more than 200,000 Billikens. (Also see synthetic.)

Billiken

11" Billiken marked "Horsman," composition head, teddy-bear style body, label on chest illegible.

$350-$400

Trudy

14" composition three-face Trudy by Horsman, faces changed by turning knob on top of head, wearing original dress marked "Sleepy Trudy, Weepy Trudy & Smiley Trudy."

$175-$250

Bright Star

14" Horsman "Bright Star," all composition, jointed body, all original in blue dress, white apron, straw hat, with original tag.

$225+

Jeanie
14 1/2" composition by
Horsman, marked "Jeanie
Horsman" on back of head,
cloth body, brown tin sleep
eyes, molded hair, cotton dress.
$125-$150

Nancy
20" composition Nancy
by Horsman, brown
sleep eyes, open mouth
with teeth, brown curls,
all jointed, wearing a
pink dress.
$125-$150

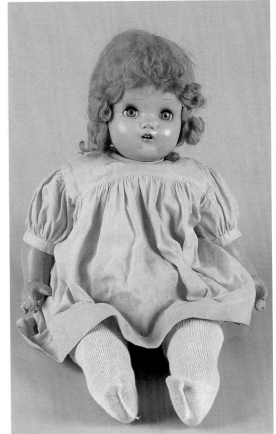

Jeanette McDonald
21" Jeanette McDonald
by Horsman, all
composition, open mouth,
brown sleep eyes, blonde
wig, all original (some
facial crazing).
$500-$550

Horsman Doll
24" composition, marked
"Horsman Doll," blue
sleep eyes, open mouth
with teeth, blonde
mohair wig, cloth body,
wearing a peach-colored
cotton dress.
$125-$200

Horsman Campbell Kids

The earliest Horsman Campbell Kids came with composition heads on cloth bodies, and were made with a flange neck. In 1914, a shoulder head was used. Outfits copied the Campbell Soup advertisements and were labeled, "The Campbell Kids/Trademark by/Joseph Campbell/Mfg. by E. I. Horsman Co." In 1929, American Character Co. acquired the license for Campbell Kids. Their all-composition version was slightly pigeon-toed. They are marked with raised lettering on the neck "A Petite Doll." Outfits were familiar Campbell Soup advertising costumes.

Horsman began to manufacture Campbell Kids again in the late 1940s. The dolls were unmarked, except for hangtags that read, "Campbell Kid/A Horsman Doll." A Canadian company, Dee and Cee, purchased the rights for the Campbell Kids in the late 1940s. The Dee and Cee dolls are similar to the Horsman Campbell Kids, with a few exceptions. Horsman eyelashes tend to be heavier and thicker; and the hair color is more orange than brown. (Also see American Character, and synthetic.)

All composition Campbell Kids share a similar face with molded and painted, bobbed hair; round, side-glancing eyes; chubby cheeks; pug nose; and closed smiling mouth.

Mary Hoyer Doll Manufacturing Co., 1925 to 1970s

Located in Reading, Pa., Mary Hoyer owned and operated a yarn shop, selling a wide variety of yarns and craft supplies through her mail-order business. She wanted a small, slim doll to use as a model for her clothing designs. (Also see synthetic.)

Hoyer enlisted the aid of Bernard Lipfert, a doll sculptor, to design a doll for her. The Fiberoid Doll Co. in New York produced the composition dolls until 1946, when hard plastic became available. For more information, see Mary Hoyer's book, Mary Hoyer and Her Dolls (Hobby House Press, Inc., 1986).

Mary Hoyer
14 1/2" Mary Hoyer composition girl, marked in a circle on her back, "The Mary Hoyer Doll," blue sleep eyes, wearing a pink dress.

$400-$500

Ideal® Novelty and Toy Co., founded 1902

Morris Mitchom and A. Cohn founded the company initially to produce Mitchom's teddy bears.

Ideal was one of the few large companies that made its own composition dolls. The company pioneered the so-called "unbreakable" dolls in America. American Character, Arranbee, Eugenia, and Mary Hoyer were among Ideal's customers. (Also see synthetic.)

Ideal Doll
17" composition, marked "Ideal Doll" on head, cloth body, closed mouth.
$125+

Ideal Doll
21" composition, marked "Ideal Doll USA," brown sleep eyes, brown hair, wearing original olive-green dress.
$100-$150

Ideal Doll
27" composition doll, marked "Ideal Made in USA" on head, reddish brown hair, sleep eyes, wearing yellow taffeta dress with ribbon lace trim and bows. (Unusual this size.)
$275+

Deanna Durbin
21" Deanna Durbin, marked "Ideal" on back, blue sleep eyes, open mouth with teeth, white cotton dress with green dots may be original.
$500-$550

Shirley Temple
12" composition Shirley Temple by Ideal, marked on head "11 Shirley Temple" and on back "Shirley Temple," with suit tag marked "Genuine Shirley Temple Doll, Ideal Toy Corp."
$650+

Shirley Temple
13" composition Shirley Temple by Ideal, marked on head "Shirley Temple Ideal Co.," and on back "Shirley Temple 13," brown sleep eyes, with net for hair, wearing original white dress with black dots and black trim, and black shoes.
$550+

Shirley Temple
13" composition Shirley Temple, marked "Ideal Genuine Shirley Temple," composition jointed body, in original dress labeled "Genuine Shirley Temple."
$500-$550

Shirley Temple
16" composition Shirley Temple, probably by Ideal, marked on head "Shirley Temple 16," open mouth with teeth, sleep eyes, wearing original plaid cotton dress and shoes.
$550+

Shirley Temple
17" composition Shirley Temple by Ideal, marked on head and back, jointed body, blonde curly hair, wearing original blue and white dotted dress.

$600+

Shirley Temple
18" composition Shirley Temple by Ideal, marked "Shirley Temple" on head and "Shirley Temple 18" on back, brown eyes, open mouth with teeth, wearing original white dress, shoes and socks.

$650+

Shirley Temple
19" composition Shirley Temple, marked "Shirley Temple Ideal" on head, sleep eyes, red and white dotted dress, redressed.

$650+

Shirley Temple
24" composition Shirley Temple, marked "Shirley Temple Ideal" on head, brown flirty eyes, open mouth with teeth, redressed.

$750+

Other Composition Dolls

Three 7 1/2" Dionne Quints, unmarked, probably made in Japan, all composition jointed babies, painted eyes and mouths, molded hair, wearing organdy dresses.

$100 each

8" composition shoulder head, German, painted black eyes and painted teeth, cloth body, felt clothes, all original, slight crack to face.

$50-$75

10" composition Patsy-type, marked "Germany," painted eyes, molded hair, wearing a gold-colored coat and hat; all original.

$90-$125

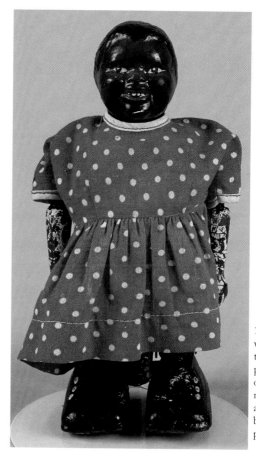

10" composition "ramp walker" black mammy that pushes a baby buggy, painted eyes and mouth, one arm has spring mechanism at elbow to allow it to hold onto buggy, wearing original polka-dot dress.

$75+

Four 11" Dream World and National Costume Doll Co. dolls, 1940s, in various original costumes.

$120+ each

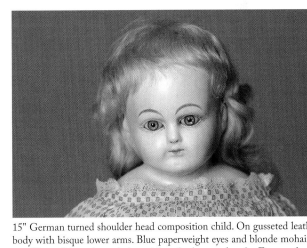

Four 11" Dream World and National Costume Doll Co. dolls, 1940s, in various original costumes.

$120+ each

13" unmarked composition doll, made in Canada to resemble a Dionne Quint, brown tin eyes, jointed body, wearing original pink dress and bonnet; good condition.

$100+

15" German turned shoulder head composition child. On gusseted leather body with bisque lower arms. Blue paperweight eyes and blonde mohair wig. Dressed in antique clothes with early shoes and socks. Fine crack to composition on left cheek and a small one below right eye. Body is in excellent condition.

$300-$400

Two Peruvian composition figures, taller 15", wearing printed and painted embroidered clothing, all original.

$75+ each

15 1/2" composition "Toni-type," blue-gray eyes, closed mouth, blonde wig, silver and blue taffeta dress and hat, redressed.

$125+

Composition Dolls

16" composition head, molded hair, brown sleep eyes, closed mouth, resembles Patsy Joan doll, dress possibly original.

$100-$125

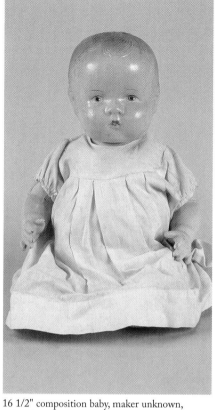

16 1/2" composition baby, maker unknown, painted eyes and mouth, original 1930s dress.

$60-$100

18" composition carnival doll, jointed at shoulders, painted eyes and mouth.

$75+

18" composition doll, unmarked, jointed, with blue tin sleep eyes, blonde wig, original rose-colored velveteen dress.

$100+

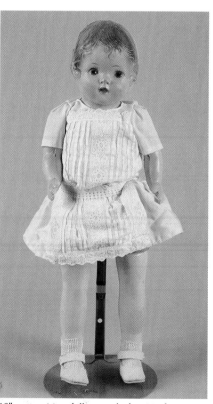

18" composition doll, unmarked, painted eyes and mouth, cotton body stuffed with excelsior, wearing a white dress.

$65-$85

18" composition girl, unmarked, jointed body, blue sleep eyes, closed painted mouth, blonde mohair wig, wearing a pink dress.

$75-$120

18" composition Baby Shirley Temple, marked "Shirley Temple" on head, blue flirty eyes, molded hair, open mouth with teeth, wearing original clothes and shoes.

$900+

19" composition, unmarked, "Judy Garland-type," bent arms, gray sleep eyes, open mouth with teeth, wearing a white cotton dress with blue trim.

$125+

20" composition swivel head, marked "UNIS FRANCE 301" on back of head (UNIS is an acronym for the Union Nationale Inter-Syndicale, a mark found after 1915 on various French dolls produced by the Société Française de Fabrication des Bébés et Jouets), brown glass stationary eyes, open mouth with teeth, jointed composition body, wearing a rose-colored satin dress, brown boa, brown lace stockings, and leather shoes.

$550+

21" composition head and limbs, marked "Made in Germany," blue sleep flirty eyes, open mouth and teeth, dressed in a blue knit suit and old leather shoes.

$200-$250

21" composition shoulder plate and limbs, unmarked (possibly Effanbee or Ideal), blue sleep eyes, open mouth with teeth, cloth body, wearing a blue print dress.

$75+

21" composition baby, unmarked, molded hair, brown sleep eyes, open mouth, cloth body, wearing a yellow dress.

$75-$110

21" composition, unmarked, jointed, brown sleep eyes, closed mouth, wearing bridesmaid dress.
$200-$225

22" black composition, cloth body with composition hands, plastic-covered flirty eyes, molded hair, wearing a white cotton dress.
$100+

22" composition Shirley Temple, brown sleep eyes, original wig, redressed.
$700+

23" composition head and limbs, unmarked, brown tin sleep eyes, open mouth and teeth, wearing original white dress and sunbonnet; some crazing.
$100-$125

23" composition, marked "Germany 352W7," brown flirty sleep eyes, open mouth and tongue, molded hair, cloth body, wearing blue knit suit.
$400+

24" composition head, made in Italy (possibly Luigi Furga & Co., founded 1872), blue flirty eyes, closed mouth, jointed composition body (except for elbows and knees), wearing a brown taffeta dress and hat.
$250+

Metal-Head Dolls

The chief manufacturing center for metal-head Dolls was in Germany at Nossen, Saxony. The familiar tin heads, dating from the turn-of-the century to the 1930s, were cut and stamped from sheet metal, then welded together. These inexpensive heads were sold separately, usually as replacements for the easily broken doll heads of bisque or china. This explains why metal heads are found on various body types. The painted or enameled surfaces are easily chipped and cracked.

Sleep eyes
13" metal shoulder head, unmarked, blue tin sleep eyes, composition hands, closed mouth, wearing a cream-colored baby dress.

$150+

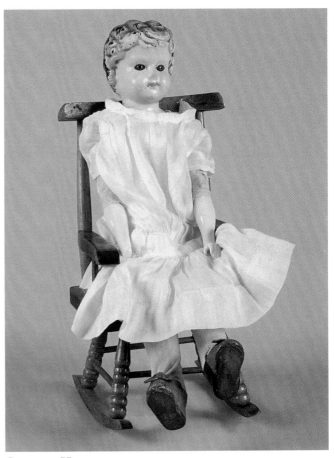

Germany 55
13" metal shoulder head, marked "Germany 55," blue glass eyes, closed mouth, cloth body, china hands, wearing a white cotton dress and leather shoes.

$175+

Germany
14" metal shoulder head, marked "Germany" on back shoulder plate, blue threaded glass eyes, open mouth with teeth, brown wig, china hands, kid body, wearing a white cotton dress and black shoes.
$175+

Minerva
16" metal shoulder head, marked "Minerva" on chest, painted blue eyes, closed mouth, composition hands, wearing a maroon hooded cape with lace dress.
$100+

Minerva
17" metal shoulder head, marked "Minerva" on chest, painted blue eyes, open mouth blonde hair, wearing a black cape with fur collar.
$150+

Shoulder Head
19" metal shoulder head, unmarked, blue stationary glass eyes, open mouth, blonde wig, leather body, bisque hands, wearing a cotton dress, pink socks and shoes; all original, near mint, seldom found in this condition.
$250+

Papier-mâché and Wax Dolls

These two types of dolls are combined here because the two materials are frequently paired on the same figure.

Papier-mâché

Various manufacturers—mostly German—made doll heads using papier-mâché. A 19th century dictionary defined papier-mâché as "a tough plastic material made from paper pulp containing a mixture of sizing, paste, oil, resin, or other substances or from sheets of paper glued and pressed together." The wood and rag fibers in paper were responsible for much of early papier-mâché's strength.

Papier-mâché, carton paté (French), and holz-masse (German) are interchangeable terms for this paper-based material. Such dolls were individually handmade as early as the 16th century, but the development of the pressure-mold process in the early 1800s allowed papier-mâché dolls to be mass-produced.

Wax

Wax Dolls were produced as early as the Middle Ages in Italy and other parts of Europe. There are three types: wax-over dolls, poured-wax dolls, and reinforced-wax dolls. The most frequently found problem with wax dolls is restoration. A network of minute age lines on an original surface is always more desirable than a newly re-waxed surface. If the surface is perfectly smooth with no cracks, dents, or scuff marks, chances are it has been re-waxed.

Occasionally someone will try to "fix" a wax doll by re-melting it (perhaps with hot spoons or a curling iron) or by having the head re-dipped. Attempts at restoration may be detected by looking for dirt embedded in the wax. A clear wax outer layer on a poured wax doll is another sign, since the original wax was tinted. When re-waxing a doll, clear wax is often used as a sealing coat.

Wax-Over Dolls

Wax-over dolls were made by various companies in England, France, and Germany during the 1800s and into the early 1900s. While dolls of many different materials were waxed over, papier-mâché or composition were the most frequently used.

An article published in the February 1875 edition of St. Nicholas magazine describes the process as follows: "... a frightful looking object she is, with color enough for a boiled lobster. When she has received her color and got dry...she proceeds to the next operator who is the waxer. In the kettle is boiling clear white beeswax, and into it Miss Dolly has been dipped, and is being held up to drain. If she had been intended for a cheap doll, she would have received but one dip, but being destined to belong to the aristocracy of the doll world, she received several dips, each one giving her a thin coat of wax, and toning down her flaming complexion into the delicate pink you see. The reason she was painted so red...is that she may have the proper tint when the wax is on. And now comes the next process, which is coloring her face. In this room is a long table with several workmen, each of whom does only one thing. The first one paints Miss Dolly's lips and sets her down on the other side of him. The next one takes her up and puts on her eyebrows. The third colors her cheeks. The fourth pencils her eyelashes, and so she goes down the table, growing prettier at every step..."

By the 1880s, paraffin or "ozocerite" (sometimes called

ader wax, earth wax, mineral wax, or "ozokerite"), made from the residue of petroleum, was used instead of beeswax. The presence of beeswax can usually be detected by its distinct odor. Although not nearly as lifelike as the poured-wax or reinforced-wax dolls, the wax-over dolls have generally survived in better condition.

Poured-Wax Dolls

Poured-wax dolls are extremely lifelike, and by the mid-1800s, such dolls were being produced as toys, but with price tags that limited their purchase to a privileged few.

The time required to make a poured-wax doll was lengthy. First, a clay sculpture was crafted and a plaster of Paris mold was made. This was accomplished by burying the clay head halfway in sand and then pouring plaster over the top. When the mold hardened, it was removed from the sand. The procedure was repeated for the other half of the head. The wax, originally beeswax and later paraffin, was placed in a cloth sack and boiled in water. It was then skimmed and placed in another sack. This purifying process was repeated at least four or five times. Purified with its high melting temperature, carnauba (a hard brittle high-melting wax obtained from the leaves of the carnauba palm) was then added to the paraffin for stability. The wax was then bleached by cutting it into strips and placing it on porcelain slabs in the sun. The wax had to be kept cool; therefore, the porcelain slabs floated on water in order to keep the wax from melting. This bleaching process took about a week.

After bleaching, the wax was colored by boiling it with lead dyes or vermilion. The melted wax was then poured into heated molds. Molds had to be heated in order to prevent ridges from forming when the wax was initially poured. After a few seconds, the two mold halves were fastened tightly together, and rotated so that the melted wax could evenly coat over the mold's entire internal surface. The molds were removed when the wax hardened. While the wax was still warm, glass eyes were inserted and the eyelids molded. Next, the features were painted and hair inserted. Finally, the completed head was attached to a cloth body with wax limbs.

Most poured-wax dolls are unmarked; occasionally a doll was stamped or engraved with a signature. The method used for attaching the hair, the finely molded eyelids, tinted wax, and well-defined poured-wax arms and legs are all indications for collectors to note.

Reinforced-Wax Dolls

Reinforced-wax doll heads are generally accepted as having been made in Germany from about 1860 until 1890. They share many characteristics with poured-wax dolls. The method for making reinforced-wax heads begins with the poured-wax process. The head is then reinforced from within by means of a thin layer of plaster of Paris or with strips of cloth soaked in a bonding agent, like composition. The intention of this reinforcement is to give the head added strength.

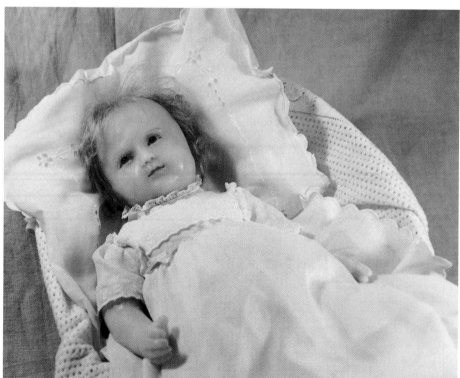

Poured-Wax

This poured-wax doll was made in England in the 1960s by an artist named Myrtle Smith. The head is on a shoulder plate, and has blue glass eyes. It is highly detailed, even to the nails on the hands and feet. Her head is turned, and the blonde human-hair lashes and brows are inserted one at a time with a hot needle. The wig tufts are inserted the same way. Clothed in old materials.

$600-$900 (Courtesy Antie Clare's Doll Hospital & Studio.)

Makers of Papier-Mâché and Wax Dolls

Ludwig Greiner, active mid-19th century

Records show Ludwig Greiner was listed as a toy maker in Philadelphia as early as 1840. In 1858, Greiner received the first known United States patent for a papier-mâché doll's head. The patent reads: "1 pound of pulped white paper, 1 pound of dry Spanish Whiting, 1 pound of rye flower [sic] and 1 ounce of glue reinforced with linen (strips of linen or silk lined the inside of the head adding strength), painted with oiled paint so that children may not pick off the paint." The heads were then given a layer of varnish, which has often served to protect the labels. A doll with the '58 patent date is known as "Early Greiner," whereas an 1872 extension date is known as a "Later Greiner."

Greiner papier-mâché heads have molded, wavy hair that gives the appearance of a high forehead and rather broad face, plus a snub nose and tight mouth.

Greiner

21" Greiner, deep shoulder head, black molded hair, brown painted eyes, cloth body, leather hands, wearing a tan cotton dress.

$900+

Greiner

12" Greiner papier-mâché with '58 label. Black hairdo with exposed ears, blue eyes and on a cloth body with leather arms. Wearing only original underwear. Right arm has split to leather at elbow. Paint is all original and untouched, minor scuff to nose.

$400-$500

Other Papier-mâché and Wax Dolls

9" German papier-mâché milliner's model with wardrobe, with curls descending onto the back of her neck. Several garments are included along with a box of miniature books. Overall condition is very good. Doll shows crazing and varnish loss to face.

$600-$700

10" papier-mâché shoulder head baby, mechanical mouth (mechanism in body controls mouth, which opens when stomach is pressed), blue stationary glass eyes, cardboard body, cloth and composition hands and feet, wearing a white baby dress and bonnet.

$100+

13 1/2" German milliner's model with long braids. All original, late 1830s. Dressed in a gauze outfit highlighted by red silk ribbon and lace. Exposed ears and long braids. Some scuffing to face.

$550-$650

Two papier-mâché dolls, one with a 10" cloth body with wood limbs, replaced right arm; the second with an 11" cloth body with wood arms and legs. Nice condition.

$200-$300/pair

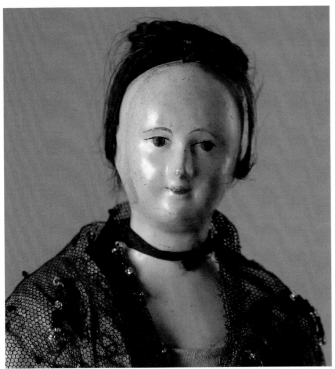

10" French papier-mâché. With painted eyes and pate with human hair attached. Wig slightly detached and original nail holes (to keep wig in place) are visible. Pink kid body (faded) and is not wearing original clothing, but has original underwear. Overall very fine original untouched condition. Small scuff to nose and some soiling to side of face.

$400-$500

Left, 14" papier-mâché composition swivel head (Kathe Kruse-type), cloth-stuffed body, painted blue side-glancing eyes, closed mouth, wearing green felt dress and black leather shoes; all original.

$350+

Right, 13" papier-mâché composition (Kathe Kruse-type), painted eyes, molded hair, cotton-stuffed joined body, wearing felt romper and shorts; all original.

$340-$400

15" French papier-mâché lady. With painted skull cap, applied human hair wig and a pink kid body (slight fading to body). Dressed in period clothing, lacking shoes. Condition is very fine with no apparent repainting to papier-mâché.

$650-$750

16" German papier-mâché lady with rare hairdo, milliner's model. Doll has molded bun in back and braided tendrils. Silk sea-foam green high-waisted dress with gathered sleeves. Very good condition, although head has crazing to papier-mâché and black-light reveals overpaint to breastplate.

$1,000-$1,200

18" papier-mâché shoulder head, painted brown eyes, blonde mohair wig, cotton-stuffed jointed body, wearing traditional German outfit of tan shorts, white shirt, red tie.

$200+

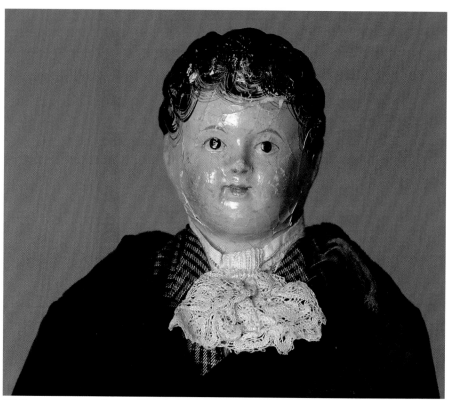

18" German papier-mâché man. Short, curly black hair with brown painted eyes and is on a French kid body. Wearing a velvet overcoat with plaid vest and wool knickers. Head has lots of crackling and lifting of surface.

$200-$300

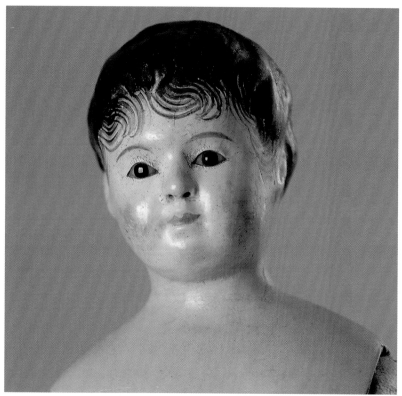

18" German glass-eyed papier-mâché man, with molded black hair and painted curls on forehead, also having pierced nostrils on a milliner-type body. Overall condition is good, there has been repair and touch-up to molded shoulder plate and head.

$650-$750

23" papier-mâché shoulder head, blue stationary eyes, blonde wig, closed mouth, composition body and hands, leather boots, wearing a white and blue print dress with white apron, and a white lace bonnet with blue ribbon.

$100+

32" papier-mâché shoulder head, brown stationary glass eyes, brown wig, closed mouth, cloth body stuffed with excelsior, composition hands and lower legs, molded socks and shoes, wearing a cream-colored lace net dress.

$80+

34" papier-mâché shoulder head, large brown stationary eyes, closed mouth, brown wig, cloth body stuffed with excelsior, composition hands and feet, wearing a pink plaid dress with lace collar.

$80+

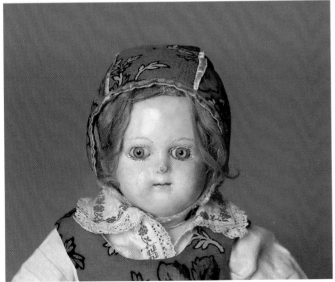

13" French wax-over papier-mâché Schmitt Bébé (Schmitt et Fils, Paris, 1863 to 1891). Dressed in regional costume. On a fully jointed and marked Schmitt body with Paris Shop label on torso. Face has scuffing and has yellowed. Body has chipping around toe area.

$500-$700

13" German wax child with trunk and wardrobe. Inset blue glass eyes, dirty blonde mohair wig, on a cloth body with squeaker in torso, and composition lower limbs. With many original costumes and some newer items. Doll is encased in a leather trunk. Overall good condition.

$350-$450

15" wax-over shoulder head, pierced ears, blonde wig, blue stationary eyes, composition arms and legs, painted shoes and socks, wearing a lavender dress.

$300+

15" two-face Bartenstein wax over papier-mâché baby (Fritz Bartenstein, after 1880). Glass inset eyes, one face is smiling, the other is open mouthed and crying. Motchmann-style body with two pull-cords; one for crier, the other to revolve head. Wax is in fair condition, having lost original luster and coloring.

$300-$350

16" wax fashion lady. Shoulder-head wax with glass inset eyes, cloth body and wax limbs. Legs have molded shoes and arms have molded gloves in place. All original, wearing a light red polished cotton gown with lace trim and sandy blonde mohair wig. Small crack to wax from eye toward ear.

$900-$1,000

17" ladies half doll, 1920s, used to cover powder boxes, etc., turned wax head with arms joined to torso by wire, bleached blonde mohair wig, wearing a skirt of beige painted net.

$100+

17" Schmitt Bebe with wax head (Schmitt et Fils, Paris, 1863-1891). Wax-over head on a marked Schmitt body, stamped on derrière with Schmitt mark and also has large oval stamp on torso. Inset blue threaded paperweight eyes, wearing antique clothing, shoes and original wig. Wax has slight roughness to nose.

$2,500-$3,000

Two 17" wax Frenchmen. Painted facial detailing, papier-mâché bodies and applied wigs. Dressed in military garb. Some discoloring to the wax faces.

$700-$800/pair

Two 17" wax Frenchmen. Painted facial detailing, papier-mâché bodies, and applied wigs. Dressed in traditional garb. Some discoloring to the wax faces, and one has a silk shirt with heavy deterioration.

$250-$300/pair

18" English wax lady. Mohair wig, blue inset eyes with detailed eyebrows and painted upper and lower eyelashes. Lower arms and legs are wax. Wearing antique, probably original clothing, which shows some stress to the fabric. Some visible hairlines on forehead and side of head.

$250-$350

18" English wax baby. Blue glass eyes and inset blonde hair on a cloth body with wax limbs. Wearing an antique christening gown and matching bonnet. Right foot missing.

$300-$400

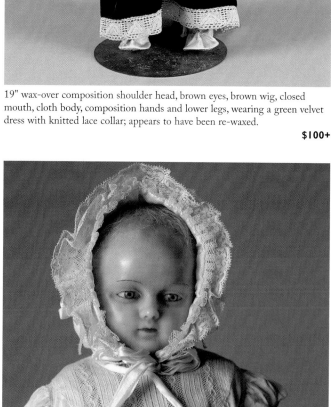

19" wax-over composition shoulder head, brown eyes, brown wig, closed mouth, cloth body, composition hands and lower legs, wearing a green velvet dress with knitted lace collar; appears to have been re-waxed.

$100+

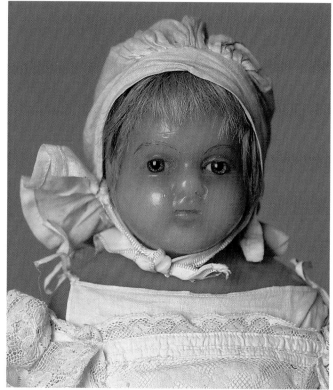

20" English wax baby signed "Lucy Peck." Blonde inset hair, blue glass eyes, and cloth body with wax lower limbs. Wearing a cotton christening outfit and matching bonnet. Some scuffing to wax, especially on arms.

$350-$400

20" English wax baby with open mouth and teeth. Inset blonde hair (somewhat sparse), cheek coloring, on a cloth body with wax lower limbs. Wearing an antique christening gown with matching bonnet. Overall very good.

$700-$800

20" English wax baby. With blue inset eyes, applied and painted hair, on a cloth body with wax lower arms and legs. Wearing an antique white cotton christening gown and lace bonnet. Pinkie missing on right hand.

$250-$350

20" English wax lady. Turned shoulder-head wax with brown inset eyes and costume with long train. Composition lower arms and lower legs with molded high-heeled shoes. Body is cloth stuffed with excelsior. Some loss to painted highlights.

$400-$450

24" English wax baby. Blue glass sleep eyes, inset hair and wax lower limbs. Wearing antique white cotton dress and matching bonnet. Left leg has collapsed inward.

$200-$300

27" glass-eyed wax shoulder-head doll with inset brown pupil-less eyes, brown curled wig and silk dress (extremely frail). On a cloth body with leather arms (probably early replacements). Has "dent" to wax below chin, paint loss to lip and face coloring.

$100-$125

Porcelain Dolls

Bisque, china, and Parian

Bisque, china, and Parian are all made of clay, feldspar, and flint. This mixture may be molded or poured, fired, painted, and fired again. Bisque is unglazed porcelain, usually with a flesh color and a matte finish. China is glazed porcelain (see China-Head Dolls). Parian is also unglazed porcelain, but without a tint (see Parian Dolls).

Pink bisque is not painted, but rather tinted pink. Painted all-bisque dolls have paint applied as a thin wash over the entire body after firing.

In fine antique dolls, bisque may appear almost translucent, whether it is used only for doll heads or for the whole figure. Though there are exceptions, early antique dolls tend to have bisque that is pale. Before 1880, most bisque heads were of the shoulder-head type, with or without a swivel. The earliest bisque, china, and Parian dolls were pressed into a mold by hand, while later examples were poured using "clay slip," a suspension of clay particles in a water solution.

Most antique French all-bisque dolls are unmarked. They usually appear smooth and delicate. A molded loop found at the base of the neck—sometimes called a "French loop" or "bell top"—allowed the head to be strung to the body. These dolls are jointed at the hip, neck, shoulder, and sometimes the elbows or knees, connected by wooden pegs, wire, or elastic, and lined with kid to cushion the parts. French all-bisque dolls usually have glass eyes, but some may be painted.

German all-bisque dolls range in size from less than 1" to well over 12" tall. Many have the head and body as one piece. If the head is a swivel neck, it may be attached with a wooden neck plug, or the neck may have holes on either side and be strung with elastic. They are often marked "Germany," and include a mold or size number; in rare instances, a paper label may be found intact on the chest.

Japanese all-bisque dolls are usually found in smaller sizes, ranging from 1" to about 8" tall. Painted features are often crude, and the bisque surface is often rough—sometimes referred to as stone or sugar bisque. Marks include "Japan" or "Nippon."

Condition

An antique bisque doll head considered to be in "excellent" condition is one without cracks, hairlines, repairs, rubs, or "wig pulls."

A line or chip in an antique bisque head that can be seen with the naked eye is considered a "crack." Chips often appear near the base of a bisque socket head.

A fine crack that occurred during the initial firing of the bisque doll is referred to as a "firing line." These are often filled with color that seeped in during the first firing. Firing lines are considered more stable than hairlines that develop later, and many collectors look upon them as minor imperfections when found on areas of an antique bisque head that are not obvious.

A fine crack that appears on an antique bisque head after initial manufacture is called a "hairline," and these may be so fine that they cannot be seen with the naked eye. Hairlines may be spotted by using either a strong magnifying glass on the outside of the head or by placing the doll's open head (without pate and wig) under a bright light. They may appear as fine threads running through the bisque. A bisque doll head with a hairline is worth less than one without, and a hairline on the face lowers the value more than a hairline on the back of the head.

Antique bisque dolls should have smooth, clear bisque. As the name implies, "pepper marks" are black specks indicating there were impurities present when the head was manufactured. Absolutely perfect bisque heads are not common, so light speckling or pepper marks in inconspicuous places are considered minor.

Collectors use the term "rub" to describe places on antique bisque where the original color has worn off. Such an area may appear white. If the rubbing occurs in an inconspicuous area, it has little effect on the value of the doll.

Some antique dolls may be found with wigs glued to the top of the bisque head. When the wig is removed by pulling it off instead of using a product to dissolve the glue, some of the paint layer may be removed with the wig. This will leave areas of white exposed bisque, generally near the crown, called a "wig pull." Such areas are usually hidden when the wig is replaced, so look closely for pull marks.

Great care must be used in cleaning porcelain. Start with a soft cloth and warm, soapy water. If this is not effective, some collectors have found success by using a wet eraser. As a last resort, try a low-abrasive bathroom or kitchen cleaner. But be careful: some cleaners contain bleach that may damage antique bodies, clothing, and wigs.

As with any valued antique, avoid displaying bisque, china, or Parian dolls in direct sunlight.

Phenix Bébé
19" Steiner Phenix Bébé (also spelled Phoenix Bébé). Even bisque, blue paperweight eyes and a fully jointed composition body. Marked on the rear of head "92." Wearing a replacement human hair wig and a French-style dress, with jacket and matching bonnet. White spot on tip of nose. Composition body is in very good original condition, with minor wear at joints.
$2,200-$2,600

Makers of Bisque Doll Heads

Henri Alexandre, 1888 to 1895

Located in Paris, the company was in existence for only a few years before being purchased by Tourrell Co., which merged with Jules Steiner in 1895. Alexandre designed the line of Phenix Bébés, of which there were 30 models. Phenix Bébés were manufactured for many years, eventually by Jules Steiner.

Henri Alexandre Bébé
17" French Henri Alexandre Bébé. Marked on rear of head "H7A" with a "5" below the crown. Closed-mouth with blue paperweight eyes, mauve eye shadowing. On a fully jointed composition French body. Wearing an antique cotton hounds-tooth dress with silk and lace trimmings, antique leather shoes, and a newer French human hair wig. Body shows signs of wear at joints and overall is somewhat soiled.
$2,300-$2,800

Alt, Beck & Gottschalck, 1854 to 1930

Based in Nauendorf, Thuringia, Germany, the company made traditional bisque child and character babies, and glazed and unglazed shoulder heads. More than 50 mold numbers have been identified, numbered between 639 and 1288. Other manufacturers, including Kestner and Simon & Halbig, may have also contributed to the A.B.G. output.

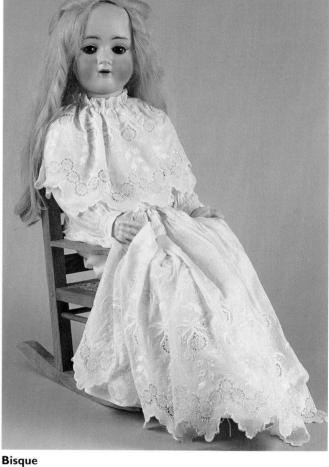

Bisque
36" bisque head, marked "Made in Germany AB 1362 6 1/2," blue stationary eyes, open mouth with teeth, replaced papier-mâché and cardboard jointed body, wearing an elaborate cotton eyelet and lace dress.

$600+

German Bisque
18" German bisque A.B.G. turned shoulder head marked with an "8." Brown sleep eyes and open mouth with teeth. On a kid body with bisque lower arms and cloth lower legs. Redressed in a lady's costume and a newer wig and hat. Thumb on right hand is broken, and there is a small scuff to left brow.

$225-$275

Louis Amberg & Son, 1878 to 1930

Located in Cincinnati, Ohio, in 1878, and in New York from 1893 until 1930, Amberg imported and manufactured bisque and composition dolls. When Joshua Amberg joined his father in 1907, the firm became Louis Amberg & Son. In 1909, Amberg was listed as the artist/owner of "Lucky Bill," the first known American doll head to be copyrighted. In the late 1920s, Amberg advertised more than 600 style numbers (including some from French and German makers). Louis Amberg & Son was sold to E.I. Horsman in 1930. (Also see cloth, composition.)

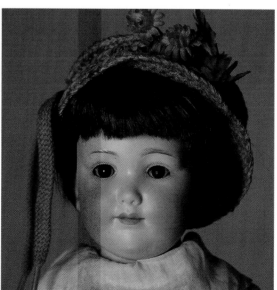

Baby Peggy
24" "Baby Peggy" By Louis Amberg. Closed-mouth character with brown sleep eyes on a "kidolene" body and bisque lower arms. Wearing a pink cotton dress, straw bonnet, antique brown leather shoes and a replaced human hair wig. Body has some sawdust leakage.

$900-$1,100

Bähr & Pröschild, 1871 to 1910

The dolls made at this porcelain factory in Ohrdruf, Germany, bear marks that help to date them. Prior to the late 1880s, dolls were marked with a mold number only. In 1888, "DEP" (a claim to registration) was added. About 1895, the initials "B&P" were included. In 1900, a crossed-swords symbol made its appearance. In 1910, when Bruno Schmidt purchased the business, Bähr & Pröschild doll marks included a heart.

Character Baby
11" bisque head character baby, marked "Bähr & Pröschild, 585 Germany," open/closed mouth, painted teeth, blue sleep eyes, jointed composition baby body, wearing a white romper with organdy and lace.
$400+

Character Baby
12" bisque head character baby, marked "Bähr & Pröschild," open mouth, stationary blue eyes, composition baby body, wearing an aqua knit outfit.
$400+

Character Baby
13" bisque head character baby, marked "585 Germany," open mouth with teeth and tongue, brown sleep eyes, composition baby body, wearing a long white cotton dress.
$500+

E. Barrois, 1844 to 1877

Located in Paris, this firm was one of the earliest manufacturers of porcelain-head dolls in France. China heads have painted eyes and hair. Most are a shoulder head, although a few socket heads on bisque shoulder plates can be found. Lady bodies are made of kid or cloth. Hands are either kid with stitched fingers, or wooden upper arms with bisque hands. Sizes range from about 9" to almost 2 feet tall. Typical markings include "E (size number) B," "E (size number) Déposé B," and "EB."

French Fashion
17" Barrois-type French fashion. Pale bisque, blue threaded paperweight eyes on a kid body with composition lower arms (left thumb missing) and legs. Original wig, which is sparse, and original camel-colored dress with dark brown fringe. Some deterioration to outfit, lacking shoes.

$1,500-$2,000

Poupée
17" French bisque Poupée Barrois-type. Stationary shoulder head fashion with blue eyes on jointed wood body with bisque lower arms. Dressed in an antique two-piece walking suit and antique underwear. Original cork pate and blonde mohair wig. Eye chips on both lower eyelids. Body has original finish to wood. One missing pinkie on right hand. Costume in frail condition.

$1,800-$2,000

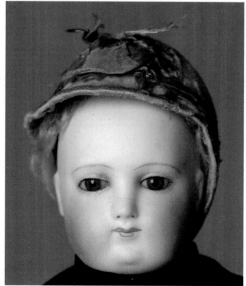

Poupée
18" French bisque Poupée Barrois-type. Shoulder head with cobalt blue eyes and fine facial detail. Kid-over-wood body with bisque lower arms, wearing a two-piece navy blue wool suit with antique blouse, underwear and hat. Three fingers on the right hand are broken off and four fingers on the left.

$2,200-$2,600

Belton-Type, after 1870

Probably manufactured in Germany in the last quarter of the 19th century, these doll heads are believed to have been made by various firms, and have an uncut pate section with one, two, or three small holes. The top of the head may be concave, convex, or even flat. Common attributes also include a good quality wig; closed mouth; paperweight eyes with long painted lashes, and pierced ears. They range in size from about 9" to 2 feet tall. Bodies are usually jointed composition with straight wrists, small hands, and long, slender wooden upper legs. They may also have a shoulder head on a kid body, with bisque hands.

Belton-Type Child
15" Belton-type 137 child. Pale bisque, dressed in an antique blue and black two-piece French-style outfit and matching bonnet (lacking shoes). On a straight-wrist, fully jointed Belton-type body. Small eye chip, one on each upper eye rim.
$600-$700

Belton-Type
9" French bisque head with flat base, Belton type, marked "3/0," two holes in head, blue glass stationary eyes, composition body, molded black shoes and socks.
$800+

C. M. Bergmann, 1888 to 1931

This firm, located in Waltershausen, Germany, specialized in ball-jointed composition bodies with bisque heads. The heads came from several makers, including Alt, Beck & Gottshalck, Armand Marseilles, Simon & Halbig and William Gobel. The dolls were distributed in the U.S. by Louis Wolf & Co., which registered some Bergmann trademarks, including "Baby Belle," "Cinderella Baby," and "Columbia."

Bisque Head
24" bisque head, marked "287 CM Bergmann, BBI Germany," green stationary eyes, open mouth with teeth, composition body with stick legs, wearing green dress and hat.

$500-$550

Character Boy
36" bisque head character boy, marked "CM Bergmann Waltershausen 1916 13," brown stationary eyes, open mouth with teeth, fully jointed body, wearing green wool outfit.

$1,200-$1,500

Bru Jne & Cie, 1866 to 1899

Founded by Leon Casimir Bru, the firm that was located in Paris and Montreuil-sous-Bois, France, is often simply called Bru. Bru dolls fall into three categories: The Bébé on a kid body, the Bru Doll on a wood-and-composition body, and the Fashion Ladies, or Poupee de Modes.

The Societe Francaise de Fabrication des Bébés et Jouets, founded in 1899, continued to make Bru Dolls and Bébés. The S.F.B.J. later resurrected the Bru trademark, in 1938 and 1953.

Bébé Teteur (Bru Nursing Bébé): bisque socket head; kid-lined bisque shoulder plate; kid body with bisque lower arms; kid-covered, metal upper arms and legs; carved wooden lower legs or jointed wood-and-composition body; skin wig; paperweight eyes; mouth opened in to an "O" with hole for nipple; mechanism in head sucks liquid as key is turned; appropriately dressed; typically marked "Bru June N T."

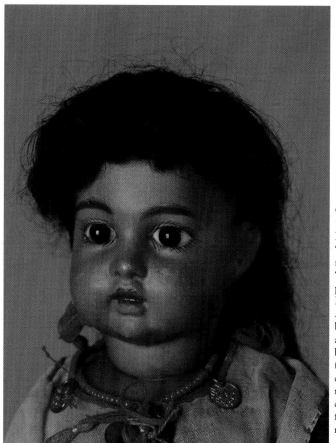

Circle Dot Bru
13" Brown Circle Dot Bru. Marked with "CIRCLE DOT" and number "3" on head, "BRU JNE" on shoulder plate and stamped "BÉBÉ BRU #3" on leather torso. Amber eyes with even brown bisque, bisque arms and chevrot-style body and wearing antique (possibly original) ethnic clothing. 1" hairline from right ear to crown. Minor cheek scuffs and a pin flake to lower right eye rim.

$4,000-$4,500

Bru Fashion
13 1/2" all original Bru fashion. Swivel-neck (marked "C" on head) on a gusseted kid body with blue paperweight eyes and fine pale bisque. Dressed in a sea-foam green silk gown with pleated train; white feather boa, outfit adorned with lace and flowers. Original wig and brown leather boots. Outfit frail with slight fraying on arms.

$3,200-$3,700

Nursing Bru Bébé
15" bisque nursing Bru Bébé. Original blonde mohair wig, cork pate, and original mechanism in head is still intact. Lace and gauze baby costume with pink silk ribbons is original. Layers of undergarments and original buttoned diaper. On a fully jointed composition French body. Body retains original finish with normal wear. Earring loop is chipped on left ear.

$6,000-$7,000

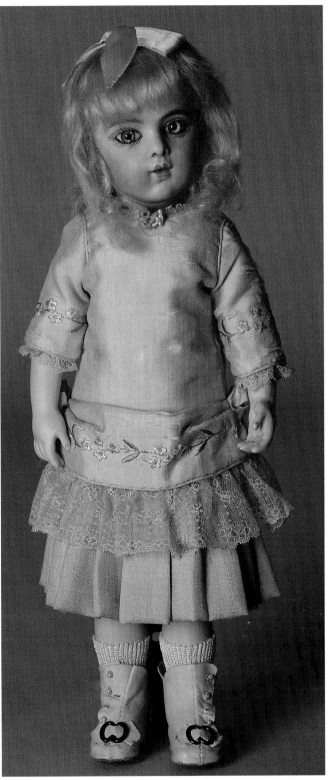

Bru Jne Bébé
15" Bru Jne #4 Bébé. Molded tongue with deep mottling, chevrot body and blue paperweight eyes. Blonde mohair wig and replaced French-style clothing. Restoration to crack running from top of head between left eye and ear, under chin and continuing behind the right ear to the top of head. Paint spray has been removed, exposing a small white line (1/4" wide) starting at lower ear and continuing under chin; this is not visible when wig is in place. Extra kid has been glued on at elbow joints. Leather body overall in good condition, wood lower legs have been repainted.

$3,000-$4,000

Bru Poupée

15" French bisque Bru Poupée. Signed on shoulder plate. Swivel neck and stationary blue eyes, on a gusseted leather body. Dressed as an older child in a blue mariner's costume with detailed red stockings and red pocketbook with comb. Original human hair wig and antique ivory leather shoes. Light speckling across brows.

$1,800-$2,200

Bru Poupée

15" French bisque Bru Poupée. Blue eyes, on a kid body with jointed bisque lower arms and kid over wood upper arms. Dressed in an antique wool coat with hood and linen skirt with blue polka dots. Original cork pate and replaced human hair wig. Leather body with split seam in buttocks.

$2,500-$3,000

Bru Poupée

15" French bisque Bru Poupée. Marked on shoulder plate. Blue glass eyes, wearing a two-piece heavy cotton antique walking suit and antique leather high-button boots. On a fully articulated straight-wrist wooden body, with human hair wig. Light speckling on chin and forehead, body finish has a lot of wear, especially to legs.

$4,000-$4,500

Oriental Fashion

15" oriental fashion attributed to Bru. Original human hair wig, on a fully jointed wood fashion body. Costumed in silk embroidered kimono and straw hat with wax flowers, antique underwear and brown leather boots. Toes are missing.

$9,000-$11,000

Nursing Bru

17" French bisque nursing Bru. Labeled Bru body with wood lower legs and replaced bisque arms. Large blue paperweight eyes and blonde mohair wig with cork pate. Wearing antique white baby gown with bottle attached. Bisque has some light dusting and inherent mold line under chin and a small scuff to right brow. Paperweight eyes are old replacement. Leather body in good condition. Lower legs are repainted.

$2,800-$3,200

Bru Poupée

16" French bisque Bru-type Poupée. Pale bisque and gray paperweight eyes. On a French leather body, with original blonde mohair wig. Dressed in gold and blue print silk costume in frail condition. Antique underwear and original black high-heeled slippers. Wear to hands, fine speckling to bisque.

$2,400-$2,800

Brevete Fashion

17" French Brevete fashion. Stiff neck with blue paperweight eyes, pale bisque and on a marked gusseted kid body with china lower arms. Body has blue stamp "BREVETE SGDG" and "D-D" in oval. Wearing older replacement clothing, and has a short blonde curly wig and antique leather boots. Some brown speckles to bisque.

$2,800-$3,300

Bru Jne 6

18" Bru Jne. No. 6. With tongue on a chevrot body and paper label on chest. Head and shoulder plate have had repair/restoration and finger on left hand has also been repaired. Marked "Bru Jne. 6" shoes, wearing contemporary clothing.

$5,500-$6,000

Bru Jne

19" French bisque Bru Jne Bébé. Molded brows and brown paperweight eyes. Peaches and cream bisque and well-defined tongue. Wearing original costume including marked Bru shoes, original chemise, and original blonde mohair wig. On Chevrot body with wood lower legs and bisque arms. Fine dusting to bisque on chin. Small firing crack to right shoulder plate. Rub mark on right wrist. Some moth damage to costume.

$30,000-$35,000

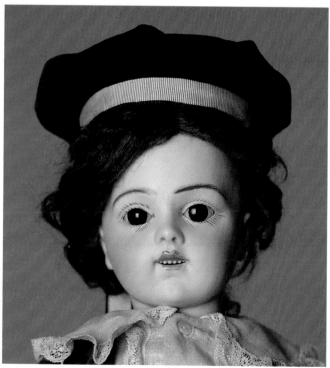

Bru Jne

21 ½" French bisque Bru Jne. R 9 boy. Brown sleep eyes; open mouth with molded teeth, brown mohair wig, dressed in a replaced brown velvet suit. Lower right lashes have a repaired chip affecting five lashes. Small scuff to lip paint. On appropriate jointed composition body.

$900-$1,200

Bru Jne Bébé

23" Bru Jne #10 Bébé. Blue paperweight eyes, even complexion bisque, on a fully jointed composition and wood Bru body (unmarked). Wearing antique French leather shoes, original underwear and appropriate French-style silk dress with matching hat. Flaking on lower arms and derriere, minor cheek scuff to lower left cheek, scuff on upper lip and minute eye flake to upper lid of left eye.

$4,000-$4,500

Cuno & Otto Dressel, 1873 to 1942

Though generations of the Dressel family operated a toy business in Germany, starting in the 18th century, the firm headed by Cuno and Otto Dressel was established in 1873. The company purchased bisque doll heads from several makers, including Ernst Heubach, Gebrüder Heubach, Armand Marseille, and Simon & Halbig, and also produced thousands of varieties of wooden and metal toys. (Also see composition, papier-mâché and wax.)

German manufacturers, such as Gebrüder Heubach and Simon & Halbig, produced Cuno and Otto Dressel's Character Dolls.

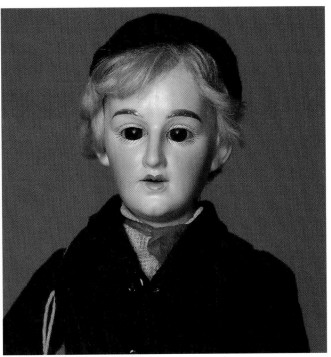

German Man

14" German character man. Marked on rear of head "M 1," possibly manufactured by Cuno & Otto Dressel. Brown set eyes with open mouth on a jointed composition body. Wearing an original man's wool outfit with matching blue cap and blonde mohair wig. Straight-wrist composition body in very fine original condition. Lacking shoes. Minor moth damage to pants.

$1,700-$2,000

Flapper

14" C.O.D. 1469 flapper lady. Dressed in appropriate lace style attire. Brown mohair wig with blue glass sleep eyes. Shoes are replacements but clothing probably original. Minor wear to body, some paint loss to ball joints.

$1,800-$2,200

German C.O.D.

23" German bisque C.O.D. marked "1349." Dressed in 1920s lady fashion, blue sleep eyes, on a fully jointed German composition body. All fingers on left hand are missing, extensive wear to lower torso.

$225-$275

Eden Bébé, 1873 to 1920s

The doll with this trade name was made by the Fleischmann and Bloedel Doll Factory, in Fürth, Bavaria, and Paris. The company became a charter member of the Societe Francaise de Fabrication des Bébés et Jouets in 1899.

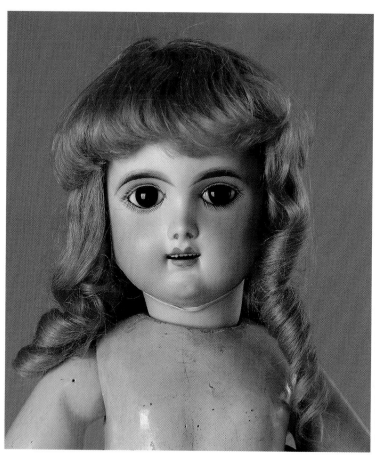

Eden Bébé
26" French Eden Bébé. Open mouth, brown paperweight eyes. On a fully jointed French composition body (right hand re-painted and chipping) and wearing some antique underwear. 2" hairline on center of forehead (covered by wig) and small mold flaw in corner of right eye.

$2,100-$2,600

French Bisque Bébés, makers unknown or attributed

14" French "M 4" Bébé. Closed-mouth doll with blue paperweight eyes and upturned lips. On a fully jointed French composition body and wearing an older lace dress and hat with an antique blonde mohair wig. Some peppering to face. Body has had some repaint (lower legs, arms and hands).

$1,200-$1,500

14" French Bébé marked "M 4." On an eight-ball-jointed, straight wrist, marked Jumeau body with blue paperweight eyes (factory eyelash miss on left lower rim) and uniform bisque. Wearing a gold taffeta dress, antique leather shoes and a replacement human hair wig (earring holes pulled through). Original spring in the head. Minor cheek blemishes, a slight nose rub and a chip to the bisque rim at rear of head. Bisque head shows pouring ripples close to rim on forehead.

$1,100-$1,400

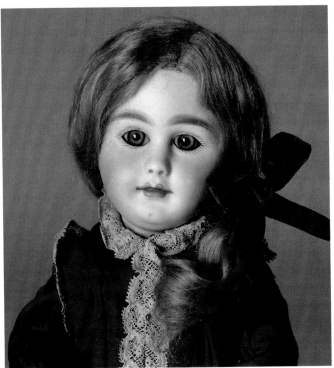

15" F.R. Bébé. Attributed to Falck & Roussel, on a fully jointed French composition style body with straight wrists and marked "FR" with number "5" underneath. Blue paperweight eyes and closed mouth. Wearing a silk Bébé dress with lace trim and antique red leather shoes. Cork pate with dirty blonde mohair wig. Minute scuff on left cheek. Rare.
$5,500-$6,000

17" French bisque Bébé marked "J·1." Attributed to Joseph Louis Joanny, 1880s, this doll has amber eyes with mauve eye shadowing and uniform bisque throughout. Wearing original blonde mohair wig and a two-piece wine silk Bébé dress, with antique matching straw hat and antique brown leather shoes. On an early French body with straight wrists. Body has overall wear with some peeling on lower arms and repair at neck socket.
$4,500-$5,000

17" French bisque Bébé marked "M 6." Pale bisque with blue paperweight eyes, on a French-style, fully jointed and composition-wood body (repainted). Wearing an antique white cotton dress and a sandy blonde human hair wig with cork pate. Body has been repainted, slight whiteness to nose tip, lacking shoes.
$1,500-$2,000

18" French bisque Bébé marked "M 8." On a marked fully jointed composition Jumeau body. Blue paperweight eyes and smooth even bisque. Repair to forehead above left eyebrow does not appear to encompass any facial features. Repair has faded and should be re-colored. Composition body has chipping to paint and flaking on leg. Torso at leg joints has been pulled.
$900-$1,100

19" French J.M. Bébé. Marked "J M" with a "2" at the crown. Blue threaded paperweight eyes and very pale bisque. On a straight-wrist eight-ball-joint French-style body. Wearing a high-waisted deep blue pinafore with ivory blouse and sandy mohair wig. Small bisque imperfection to right cheek.

$3,000-$3,500

19" Black Paris Bébé (?) Unmarked on rear of head except for the number "8." Head attached to body with an inverted wood dowel. The composition body is fully jointed and has round paper label on rear from a Paris toy store. Amber set paperweight eyes with red lips and dark eyebrows. Dressed in older velvet costume and retains original nappy hair wig and cork pate and antique leather shoes. Body in extremely fine original condition.

$5,000-$6,000

19" French bisque Bébé marked "M 7." Blue paperweight eyes and a fully jointed composition body. Wearing a maroon high-waisted dress with matching hat made of silk. Chestnut colored human hair wig. Body has wear at joints, derriere and neck has slight depression. Some deterioration to silk on dress and hat.

$1,500-$2,000

22" Paris Bébé. Blue paperweight eyes, peaches n' cream bisque, on a fully jointed and marked composition and ball-jointed body. Line from her right ear and extending a little over an inch towards her chin. Wearing antique white dress with blue ribbon trim, antique sateen blue shoes and a blonde mohair wig. Body has normal wear at joints; thighs appear to have paint restoration.

$1,800-$2,200

24" French "Bébé Francaise" #11. Blue paperweight eyes, peaches n' cream bisque. On a French jointed composition body, wearing an embroidered cotton frock highlighted by pink silk ribbons. Antique sandy brown mohair wig with bonnet, and original shoes marked "PARIS DEPOSE 11" (with bumblebee on sole). Original paint with some flaking and wear on wrists and lower arms.

$4,000-$5,000

24" French bisque Bébé marked "M 9." Large blue paperweight eyes. Bisque is even with rosy colored cheeks on a fully jointed wood body. Wearing a French-style blue dress (some fading), antique leather boots, and a sandy colored mohair wig with cork pate. Two hairlines, one on the forehead and one behind the left ear.

$1,250-$1,500

24" French bisque Bébé. Open mouth and molded teeth on a fully jointed German composition body and replaced human hair wig. Crack to the forehead with eye chips on the upper right rim. Eyes are German replacements.

$450-$550

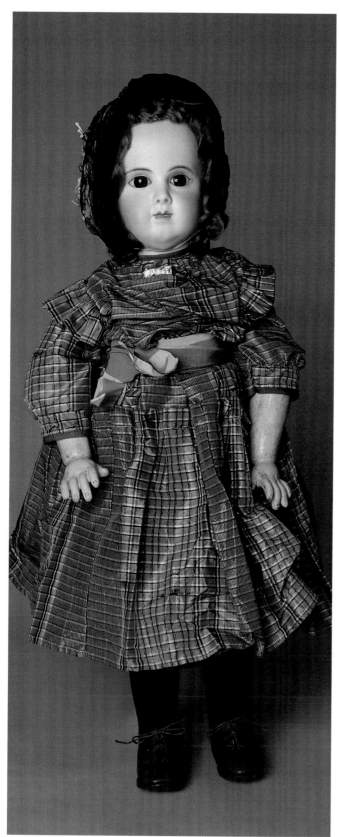

26" closed-mouth French Bébé. Possibly by E.D. (Etienne Denamur, Paris, after 1889), on a German ball-jointed body (probably Handwerck). Heavy restoration to bisque head.

$200-$250

26" French bisque marked J.M. Bébé. With golden brown eyes and soft pale bisque with lavender eye shadowing. On a fully jointed French composition and wood body with straight wrists, wearing a plaid silk lavender dress and antique children's shoes. Bisque fine, body has overall wear with some repair to feet, neck socket, and fingers.

$8,000-$9,000

French Bisque Fashion-Type

Known as Poupée de Modes or just Poupées, these adult-bodied and fashionably dressed dolls were manufactured primarily between 1860 and 1930 in France, Germany and, to a lesser degree, Austria. Bisque heads are found on bodies of cloth, kid or wood.

Kid Body Poupée de Mode: pale, fine bisque swivel head; kid-lined bisque shoulder plate; fine gusseted kid body; bisque or kid arms with stitched fingers; good wig; exquisitely painted or paperweight eyes, finely lined in black; painted lashes; feathered brows; pierced ears; closed mouth; appropriately dressed; typically marked with size number only or unmarked.

Wooden Body Poupée de Mode: pale, fine bisque swivel head; kid-lined bisque shoulder plate; attached with kid to fully articulated wooden body; wooden peg joints; good wig; paperweight eyes, finely lined in black; painted, long lashes; softly feathered brows; pierced ears; small, closed mouth; appropriately dressed; typically marked with size number only or unmarked.

The following dolls are not attributed to specific makers.

Poupée
13" French bisque Poupée. Signed on front shoulder plate (E Depose 1 B). Shoulder-head with closed mouth and dark blue eyes. Pale bisque with deep cheek color and finely painted features. On a kid fashion body, wearing antique two-piece tan-and-red costume with newer hat and wig. Wear on hands and fingers.

$1,000-$1,500

French Fashion
13" French fashion. Stiff-necked, gusseted kid with bisque arms, missing shoes. Blue paperweight eyes with pale bisque. Wearing a cream linen dress and jacket adorned with green piping. Mold flaw on right thumb, missing part of one finger on right hand. Left hand is missing forefinger.

$1,300-$1,800

Fashion
13" painted-eye fashion. Bisque shoulder-head with painted blue eyes, replaced cloth body with leather arms, and newer wig.
$400-$500

Fashion with Trunk
16" unmarked French fashion with trunk. Gusseted kid body with swivel neck and all original from wig to shoes. Trunk/wardrobe includes extra costumes, hats, a parasol, and accessories. Clothing and kid body show some wear.
$3,500-$4,500/set

Fashion

16" shoulder head fashion. Pale bisque with blue eyes on a straight kid body with bisque arms (tip of right forefinger missing). Wearing an antique brown dress with black and gold ribbon trim and French leather shoes. Wig is a human hair replacement. Firing crack on shoulder plate under dress line.

$800-$1,000

Poupée

17" French bisque Poupée. Blue glass eyes, and fine facial detailing. On a replaced cloth body with blue stitched-on boots, wearing antique two-piece red cotton dress and lace bonnet. Excellent condition.

$1,000-$1,500

Fashion Man

21" French fashion man. Stiff neck, all original with cobalt blue eyes, fine bisque, and sandy blonde mohair wig on a gusseted kid body. Dressed in a black tuxedo with vest and shirt and a beaver skin top hat with a London label inside. Lacking shoes. Brown pin spots on left eyelid.

$4,400-$4,800

Accessories

Fashion accessories. Early straw fashion hat with French label and ivory silk lining, very early ivory silk fashion slippers with little wooden heels marked "4 (T)" on the soles, three fashion dress collars, two celluloid boar bristle brushes, and fur collar.

$200-$250/set

Fulper Pottery Co., 1918 to 1921 (doll production only)

Originally founded in 1815 at Flemington, N.J., and known for its art pottery, Fulper produced bisque dolls and doll heads for less than five years.

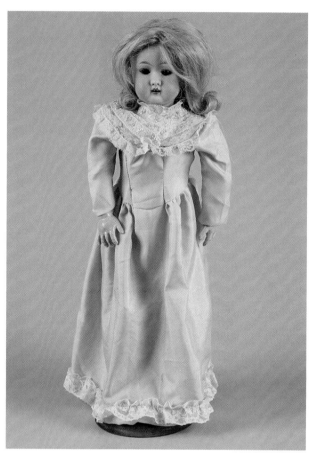

Fulper
20" bisque head, marked "Fulper Made in USA," open mouth with teeth, brown stationary eyes, fully jointed body, wearing a pink dress with white lace.
$400-$450

Francois Gaultier, 1860 to 1916

Located on the outskirts of Paris, Gaultier produced bisque doll heads for several firms, including Gesland, Jullien, Rabery & Delphieu, Simonne, and Thuiller. It later became part of The Societe Francaise de Fabrication des Bébés et Jouets.

Fashion Dolls
Left, 11" bisque shoulder head fashion doll, marked "F.G.," paperweight eyes, closed mouth pierced ears, leather hands, original wig, cloth body, redressed in purple and pink.
$1,100-$1,300.
Right, 11" bisque shoulder head fashion doll, marked "F.G.," paperweight eyes, closed mouth pierced ears, leather hands, original wig, cloth body, wearing original light green dress repaired with flowered print.
$1,100-$1,300

Black Poupée
12" black French F.G. Poupée. Dark brown bisque and brown leather kid body. Black wig, wearing a costume made of antique fabrics and striped silk and red cotton with red matching hat. Normal wear to body. Minute scuff to tip of nose and lower lip.

$1,300-$1,800

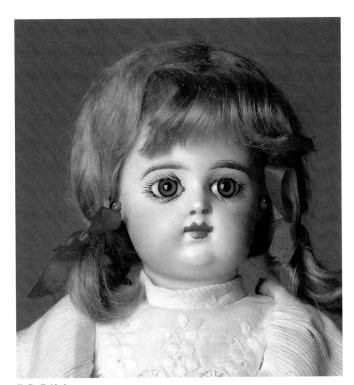

F.G. Bébé
16" F.G. Bébé. Rear of head is marked with "F.G." in scroll. Blue paperweight eyes, pale bisque, on a five-piece, jointed wrist composition body. Wearing an antique white cotton dress and blonde mohair wig. Tiny flake to lower left eye rim.

$1,400-$1,800

Fashion
17" F.G. French fashion. Blue paperweight eyes, on a Gesland body with bisque hands and lower legs. Original condition with a gauze and lace trimmed dress highlighted with silk aqua ribbons. Original blonde French mohair wig and straw hat. Lacking shoes/boots.

$3,300-$3,800

F.G. Poupée

20" French bisque F.G. Poupée. Blue spiral paperweight eyes, fine bisque. On a stockinet Gesland body with bisque limbs. Wearing an antique black walking suit with matching hat and original human hair wig with long woven braids in the back and original earrings. Minor pepper spots on cheek. Costume has some splits and wear to the skirt.

$3,000-$3,500

Bébé

21" F.G. Gesland Bébé. Marked body and rear of head "F.G." is in scroll with number "8" under scroll. Bulbous light blue paperweight eyes, even bisque and pale lips with a hint of a tongue. Wearing a newer French-type outfit with coordinating hat and jacket. Composition lower arms, legs, and shoulder plate have had paint restoration and repair.

$2,400-$2,800

F.G. Poupée

18" French bisque F.G. Poupée. Jointed wood fashion body with antique two-piece sage green silk dress with matching hat and red corset, antique underwear, and black leather shoes. Wig is replaced sheepskin. Possible early repaint to body.

$2,800-$3,300

Poupée
24" French bisque F.G. Poupée. On gusseted French leather body. Redressed in gold and blue walking suit and wearing original blonde mohair wig. Restored on face, on both lower eyes, beneath the nose and across the upper lip. Body has minor repairs.

$800-$900

Poupée
25" French bisque F.G. Poupée. Painted detail, and pale gray eyes. Original blonde mohair wig, on a gusseted French body wearing an elaborate replaced gown and white leather boots. Minor scuff to chin. Body has some small patching to gussets and fingers.

$3,000-$3,500

F.G. Fashion
29" F.G. fashion. Blue threaded paperweight eyes and fine bisque. On a gusseted kid body and wearing a floral print silk gown (minor deterioration) and antique leather shoes. Curly human hair wig with matching straw and fabric bonnet and comes with a black parasol. Repair to forehead.

$900-$1,200

Bébé
30" F.G. Gesland Bébé. Marked body, and on rear of head, "F.G." is in scroll with number "11" under scroll. Hazel eyes, pale bisque, a newer pale blue frock with tatted lace, a long light brown human hair wig and closed mouth with molded tongue. Composition body parts have been repainted. Original spring in head connecting to shoulder plate.

$3,300-$3,800

Other German Bisque, Heads and Dolls

Three bisque German Kewpies. The first is 5 1/2" tall with jointed arms, the pair is 2 1/2" tall bride and groom wearing original clothing. Overall very good. (Kewpies were first pictured in the Ladies' Home Journal in 1909, the creation of artist Rose O'Neill.)

$125-$175/set

Pair of bisque German bathing beauties: First is 6" bather with wig, in a recumbent pose holding her hands (tip of pinkie broken). Second is a 3 1/2" bather with molded hair, suit and cap. Larger figure has some distress to original knit bathing suit.

$500-$600/pair

8 1/2" German bisque 455 Googly. Blue side-glancing eyes, "watermelon" smile, jointed composition body, sandy blonde mohair wig. Clothes are older replacements. Body is antique but not original to doll.

$1,000-$1,100

13" German bisque character known as "Uncle Sam." Marked on back of head with a large "S," below that is a "1" and "Germany." Stationary blue eyes, and human hair wig and goatee. Fully jointed composition body. Overall condition is excellent. Costume has fading and soiling.

$1,200-$1,300

8 1/2" German bisque black child. Black papier-mâché body, black glass eyes, and original sparse karakul wig and black cotton dress. Face has light rubbing throughout, tips of toes are chipped.

$125-$175

15" German bisque doll marked "989." Brown sleep eyes and square-cut teeth. Original blonde curly mohair wig and redressed in red velvet boy's costume with newer shoes. On a fully jointed early straight-wrist German body. One finger has been re-glued.

$900-$1,100

16" closed-mouthed German shoulder head doll. Unmarked, wearing an antique gold cotton dress with black trim. Pale blue sleep eyes, original blonde mohair wig, and antique black leather shoes. Body has splits at hip and is leaking sawdust.

$350-$450

20" German bisque child marked "136." Wearing an early aqua silk dress with black leather shoes. Wig is a mohair replacement, with straight-wrist, eight ball-jointed body. Large brown paperweight eyes. Light speckling on forehead between brows, wig chips and mold split above ear.

$1,400-$1,600

19" German bisque child marked "136." Blue spiral eyes, on a kid body with bisque shoulder plate and appears to be all original including her blonde mohair wig and straw hat. Body is pale pink leather in excellent condition.

$1,900-$2,300

20" German bisque shoulder-head fashion. Brown glass eyes, and an older sandy brown mohair wig. Pierced ears, a painted detail, and a solid dome head. Newer cloth body, dress is extensively shredded.

$500-$600

22" German bisque shoulder-head fashion. Gray-blue paperweight eyes, closed mouth and pierced ears, original mohair wig. Kid body has bisque lower arms. Wearing a replaced black silk costume of antique fabrics with a black velvet cape and antique German shoes. Small pepper marks on forehead and chin.

$750-$850

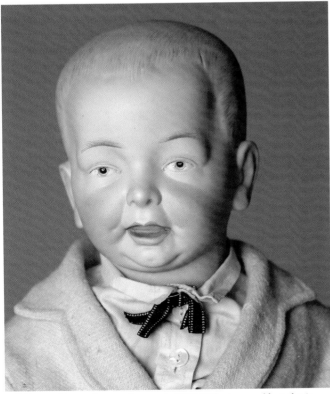

23" German bisque character boy marked "FB." Wearing an old wool suit with newer shoes. On an inappropriate jointed French body with replaced arms.

$225-$275

24" German closed-mouth doll #136. Threaded blue paperweight eyes, fine bisque, swivel neck, kid body with bisque lower arms. Wearing original blonde mohair wig with plaster pate and white cotton dress with lace inset trim. Some minor patching to kid body.

$1,400-$1,500

25" German bisque B.M. (?) 341 toddler. Dressed in green and white checked cotton dress, with white gauze pinafore and antique toddler shoes. Blonde human hair wig and poke-style green bonnet. Left pinkie is replaced, arms have crazing and hands are peeling. Lower legs are also crazed. Drip mark on chin.

$400-$500

27" bisque head boy, open mouth with painted teeth, blue sleep eyes, blonde wig, fully jointed baby body, wearing purple wool suit and hat, old leather buttoned shoes.

$1,500+

Goebel, founded 1876

Established in Bavaria by Franz D. Goebel, son William became sole owner of the porcelain factory in 1893, changing the name to William Goebel. Early Goebel bisque objects were marked with a triangle and a quarter moon. After 1900, a crown above a conjoined "W&G" was introduced.

Character Baby
14" bisque shoulder head character baby, marked with a crown and conjoined "WG" and "B5-3 Germany, Bavaria Goebel," brown sleep eyes, open mouth, composition baby body, wearing a white cotton dress.

$300+

A. Halopeau (H Mold), late 19th century

"H mold" dolls are attributed to Aristide Marcellin Halopeau of Paris. Halopeau was listed as a doll maker in the Paris annual register from 1881 until 1889.

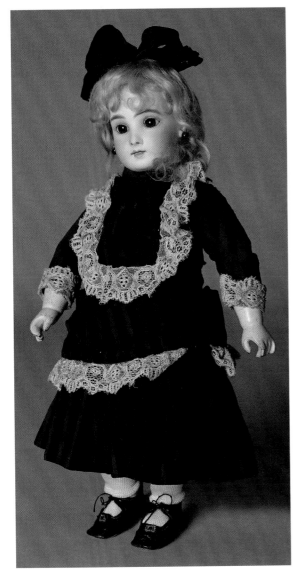

Halopeau Bébé

16" Halopeau Bébé. Marked "0 H" on rear of head. Amber paperweight eyes, pale bisque, on a French jointed wood body (probably incorrect for doll). Cork pate with blonde mohair wig, wearing an antique wine-colored, velvet striped Bébé dress. Bisque has some kiln dust throughout and tiny mold flaw at corner of nose. Rare.

$14,000-$16,000

Halopeau Bébé

18" Halopeau Bébé. Threaded blue paperweight eyes with sandy blonde mohair wig. Wearing an antique sea foam green dress with matching hat, leather boots and gloves. On a jointed composition Jumeau body. Slight nose rub.

$30,000-$35,000

Halopeau Bébé

24" Halopeau Bébé. Marked on rear of head "5 H," on a jointed, straight-wrist composition body. Threaded blue paperweight eyes, wearing an antique white cotton dress. Bisque restoration appears to be from top of eyelids up into the forehead and extending over to both ears.

$4,300-$4,800

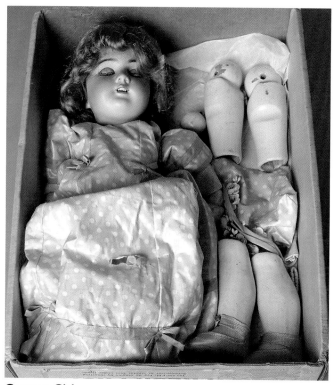

German Girl

18" German girl by Handwerck. Open mouth with brown sleep eyes and on a marked Handwerck composition body. Doll is unstrung and wig has not been removed for inspection of bisque head. Overall condition is good.

$150-$200

Heinrich Handwerck, 1876 to 1930

Founded in Gotha, Thüringia, Germany, by Heinrich Handwerck Sr. and his wife, Minna, they designed the bisque heads that were produced by Simon & Halbig. After Heinrich's death in 1902, the firm was purchased by Kämmer & Reinhardt of nearby Walterhausen.

Girl

19" girl by Handwerck, marked "Heinrich Handwerck–Simon Halbig–Germany," open mouth with teeth, brown stationary eyes, reddish hair, jointed composition body (appears new), wearing an old dress of stained apricot silk and black lace.

$450+

Bisque Head
25" bisque head, marked "Made in Germany, 12 171," body marked "Heinrich Handwerck Germany," sleep eyes, blonde wig, open mouth with teeth, composition body, wearing a blue silk dress, white stockings, black shoes.
$600-$700

Bisque Head
28" bisque head, marked "Heindrich Handwerck, Simon & Halbig, 6 Germany," brown sleep eyes, open mouth with teeth, jointed composition body, wearing a pink dress with lace.
$800-$900

Shoulder Head
24" bisque shoulder head with creamy complexion, marked "Hch H 2 JF Germany," open mouth with teeth, blue sleep eyes, kid body, chest stamped "Natural Eye lashes," wearing a peach and chiffon pink taffeta with red cherries.
$500-$600

Max Handwerck, founded 1899

Located in Walterhausen, Thüringia, Germany, Max Handwerck designed and modeled the facial molds, many of which were produced as bisque doll heads by William Goebel.

Bisque Head
25" bisque head, marked "Germany Max Handwerck," open mouth with teeth, fine brown wig, green threaded stationary eyes, fully jointed composition body, wearing a pink dress with heavy lace and a flowered headpiece.
$600-$700

Hertel, Schwab & Co., 1910 to 1930

With a factory in Stutzhaus, near Ohrdruf, Thüringia, Germany, this firm produced several dolls exclusively for the American market, including the Bye-Lo Baby for Borgfeldt; Our Baby and Our Fairy for Louis Wolf & Co., and the Jubilee Dolls for Strobel & Wilken.

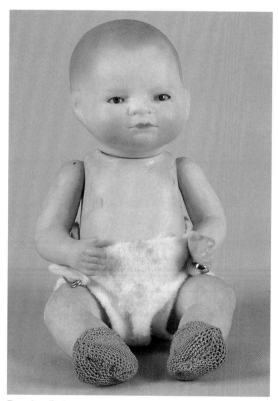

Bye-Lo Baby
6 1/2" Bye-Lo Baby, marked "Grace Storey Putnam Germany Bye-Lo," blue stationary glass eyes, diaper, and booties.
$650-$750

Bye-Lo Baby
16" Bye-Lo Baby. Marked, "Grace Storey Putnam," celluloid hands, original cloth body, blue sleep eyes, wearing white christening gown.

$900-$1,100

Ernst Heubach, 1887 to 1932

This manufacturer of bisque dolls was located in Köppelsdorf, Germany. In 1919, Heubach and Armand Marseilles merged, but later split in 1932. Dolls marked "Heubach Koppelsdorf" were produced between 1919 and 1932. Other marks include a horseshoe, the initials "E.H," and mold numbers.

Bisque Head
9" bisque head, marked "Heubach Koppelsdorf, 321-9110 Germany," blue sleep eyes, open mouth with teeth, composition baby body, brown wig, wearing a white cotton and lace dress.

$250-$300

Bisque Head
14 1/2" bisque head, marked "250 8/0 Heubach Koppelsdorf, Thuring," fully jointed composition toddler body, stationary eyes, open mouth with teeth, wearing a blue snowsuit.

$180-$225

Toddler
18" bisque head character toddler, marked "Heubach Köppelsdorf, 30-2 Germany," brown stationary eyes, open mouth with teeth (repaired lip), composition toddler body, wearing a light pink dress and bonnet.

As is, $200 to $250; if perfect, $400+

Shoulder Head
21 1/2" bisque shoulder head, marked "Heubach Köppelsdorf," blue stationary eyes, open mouth with teeth, kid body, wearing a cream-colored silk pleated dress with pink ribbon.
$300-$350

Bisque Head
27" bisque head, marked "Heubach Koppelsdorf 250-6 1/2 Germany," open mouth with teeth, blue stationary eyes, blonde wig, jointed composition body, wearing a white silk dress.
$500-$550

Bisque Head
26" bisque head, marked "Koppelsdorf Thuring," sleep eyes, jointed body, redressed for historical display.
$400-$500

Gebrüder Heubach, founded 1840

Heubach is not known to have made doll heads until about 1910, though the Heubach family bought an established porcelain factory in Lichte, Thüringia, Germany, in 1840. In addition to mold numbers, artist or sculptor initials may be included in the markings.

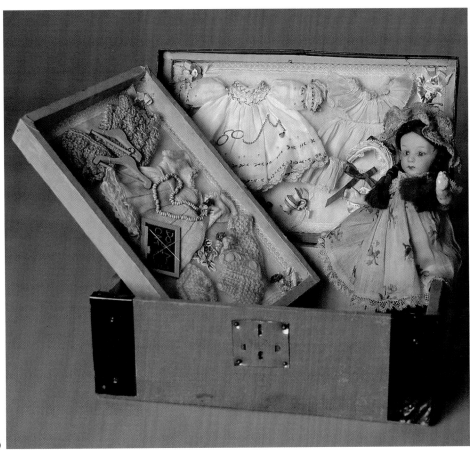

Doll with Trunk

7" Heubach character doll with trunk. Closed mouth, with blue glass eyes, jointed German composition body with bent arms and straight wrists, wearing gauze print dress and brown mohair wig in braids. Accompanied by trunk mounted with wardrobe and accessories. Minor wear at joints and small repair to neck socket.

$600-$700

Heubach

8" all bisque, marked "Heubach 95583," intaglio eyes; painted hair, socks and shoes; pink crocheted dress.

$750-$850

Laughing Twins

8 1/2" dome-head bisque laughing twins, marked "3/0 HEUBACH, Germany," all-bisque jointed bodies, intaglio eyes, both wearing cotton suits.

$900-$1,000 each

Bisque Dome Head
11 1/2" bisque dome head, marked "0 Germany Gebrüder Heubach," blue intaglio eyes, closed mouth, (professional repair to head), wearing a blue wool suit and cap.

$350+

Character
14" Gebrüder Heubach 6969 character. Original provincial outfit (lacking shoes) with blue glass sleep eyes and fine bisque. Composition neck socket on body has been repaired.

$1,200-$1,600

Laughing
15" Heubach 5636 laughing character. Blue glass sleep eyes, fine bisque and an open mouth with two molded teeth. On a German ball-jointed composition body with a brown mohair wig and antique clothing. Slight scuff underneath chin.

$2,000-$2,500

Character Girl
16" Heubach 7407 character girl. Brown sleep eyes, on ball-jointed composition body. Eye chip on lower left rim and hairline on rear of head going into a "Y." Doll is loosely strung and has replaced human hair wig.

$650-$750

Character Child

17" German bisque Heubach character child marked 8192. Antique blue gingham dress, original underwear, replaced newer shoes, and a blue straw hat. Wig is a human hair replacement, with fully jointed composition body. Normal wear to finish.

$900-$1,100

Smiling Lady

18" Gebrüder Heubach smiling lady 7925. All original turned shoulder head with original outfit (frail); wig is replacement. Composition lower arms and legs (molded socks and shoes) on a cloth body. Unusual this size. Overall condition is very fine.

$1,600-$1,800

Pouty Character

20" Heubach 7374 pouty character. Blue glass sleep eyes, on a German ball-jointed composition body (finish on lower legs not consistent with remainder of body). Wearing an antique white dress highlighted with pink ribbons, a sandy brown human hair wig with braids over the ears, and antique leather shoes. Bisque has some light brown speckling throughout.

$2,000-$2,500

Huret, second half of the 19th century

Based in Paris, Maison Huret was known for its gusseted kid and articulated wooden bodies. In 1861, it patented a socket swivel neck. Huret fashion dolls may also have china or tinted porcelain heads.

Huret Child

18" Huret child. On a fully articulated wood body. Light blue threaded paperweight eyes and closed mouth. Wearing an antique blue gingham dress with silk ivory blouse, curly blonde lamb's wool wig, antique watch and chain. Body has been stripped of paint and several fingers have been replaced.

$13,500-$14,500

Huret Fashion

18" marked, painted-eye Huret fashion. Swivel neck, painted cornflower eyes. Leather torso has the "Huret" stamp and address of the firm. Wearing antique costume with black silk slippers (heels marked "T" on the sole). With purchase provenance. Gutta percha arms and jointed lower legs have had repair and repainting. Mohair wig is a later replacement.

$10,000-$12,000

Jumeau, founded early 1840s

Pierre Francois Jumeau began manufacturing dolls in Paris and Montreuil-sous-Bois, France, in about 1842, in a partnership called Belton & Jumeau.

There are several Jumeau doll head markings. The most commonly found mark is the "Tete Jumeau" stamp and a red artist check mark. Earlier Jumeaus can be found marked "E.J." with a size number. The rare, long-faced Jumeau, as well as other portrait Jumeaus, are marked with a size number only.

DEP Bébé
10" all original Jumeau DEP Bébé with trunk, German-made for French market. Impressed "DEP" and rubber-stamped "Jumeau" on rear of head. On a fully jointed French-style composition body, wearing antique lace dress, blue leather shoes, and white fleece coat and hat. Cork pate, original mohair wig, and brown glass sleep eyes. Included assorted outfits. Overall condition is very fine, some repair and touch-up to lower legs.

$1,400-$1,500/set

Portrait Jumeau
11" second series portrait Jumeau. Brown paperweight eyes on a straight-wrist, eight-ball-jointed Jumeau body, marked with a "3" on rear of head. Brown French mohair wig, antique white dress, and French shoes. Minor wear to joints, wig is somewhat sparse.

$3,000-$3,500

Tete Jumeau
12" Tete Jumeau #3. Blue paperweight eyes, on a fully jointed and marked composition Jumeau body. Replacement (but old) maroon satin dress and antique undergarments. Minor wear at joints. Some paint and composition loss to right forearm. Wig is a newer replacement, lacking shoes.

$4,000-$4,500

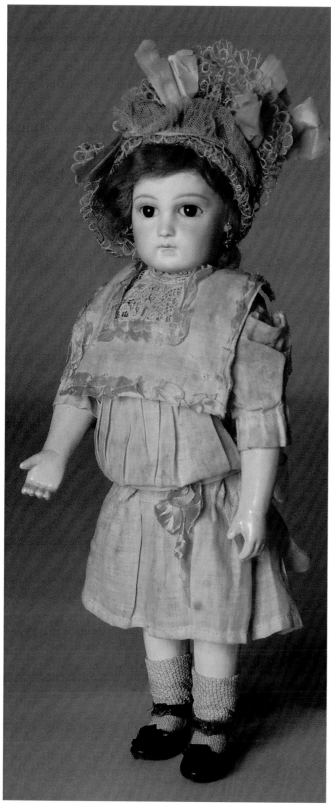

Jumeau Portrait

15" first series Jumeau portrait. Marked with "2/0," amber paperweight eyes with mauve eye shadowing, pale bisque on eight-ball-jointed body marked Jumeau. Wearing antique white low-waisted gauze dress and matching hat. Original cap to skin wig (lacking hair, but is now wearing sandy brown mohair wig). Jumeau shoes are marked "Jumeau Bébé Depose #6." Doll loosely strung, original cap to skin wig has not been removed from head.

$8,000-$9,000

Portrait Jumeau Bébé

13" second series portrait Jumeau Bébé. Brown paperweight eyes, wearing her original pale green silk outfit. Original French mohair wig, wire-frame lace hat and original spring in head. On a straight-wrist, eight-ball-jointed Jumeau body (minor wear and paint loss to fingers). Lacking shoes.

$2,500-$3,000

Jumeau Portrait
19" French bisque Jumeau portrait. Large almond eyes and heavy mauve shadowing. On a German leather body with bisque arms dressed in antique beaded ivory silk wedding gown with original satin shoes. Newer auburn mohair wig. Crack beginning at the crown above the right ear, wrapping around through the mouth, and coming out to the left ear. Body is in good condition.

$3,000-$3,500

Tete Jumeau
17" Tete Jumeau #7 with original box. Pale bisque and brown paperweight eyes on a fully jointed and marked composition Jumeau body. Original print dress with hat, cork pate, spring in head, original marked Jumeau shoes, and blonde mohair wig. Minor wear to body, manufacturing flaw on right cheek going from lower ear, curving up towards nose.

$5,200-$5,800

Déposé E9J
19" Déposé E9J doll. Blue paperweight eyes and fine bisque on a straight-wrist, eight-ball-jointed Jumeau (unmarked) body. Wearing antique shoes, a pale green dress, large bow on the back and a pale green bonnet. Original spring in head. Minor wear and paint loss at body joints.

$9,000-$10,000

Tete Jumeau

19" Tete Jumeau #8. Blue paperweight eyes, open mouth, on a stamped, fully jointed Jumeau composition body. Wearing an older pink dress and a replacement French human hair wig. Slight whiteness to nose. Wear and chipping at all joints.

$1,800-$2,200

Déposé Jumeau

19" incised Déposé Jumeau #8. Amber paperweight eyes on a straight-wrist fully jointed and marked Jumeau body. Extensive restoration to head, but still retains original spring connecting head to torso. Wearing newer style clothes and wig. Restoration primarily on forehead and bridge of nose.

$1,000-$1,300

Jumeau Poupée

19" French bisque Jumeau Poupée. Blonde mohair wig and painted lashes. On a French kid body, and wearing a burgundy silk and velvet walking suit. Couple of small holes on legs. Minute eye chip on her right lower rim.

$1,800-$2,200

Tete Jumeau

22" Tete Jumeau #9. Blue paperweight eyes, on a straight-wrist eight-ball-jointed composition body. Wearing a newer French-style dress with French human hair wig. Forehead appears to have two to three pieces glued back in, crack extending into doll's right eyebrow. Otherwise, all facial features are intact and no restoration has taken place.

$1,200-$1,500

Tete Jumeau
22" Tete Jumeau #10. Bisque featuring amber eyes on a Jumeau ball-jointed composition body. Wearing a silk taffeta print dress and an older human hair wig with coiled braids covering each ear. Wear to joints.
$1,600-$1,700

Jumeau Bébé
22" French Jumeau Bébé marked "R.9.R." Closed-mouth with blue paperweight eyes and uniform bisque on an eight-ball-jointed Jumeau composition body. Wearing a newer dark blue French-style dress with a curly human hair wig and marked antique French leather shoes (frail condition). Body has been repainted, otherwise overall condition is very fine.
$3,000-$3,500

Tete Jumeau
23" open mouth Tete Jumeau #10. Blue paperweight eyes with pale bisque and open mouth. Wearing a white dress on a fully jointed French composition body. New wig, lacking shoes. Hairline on forehead and hairline/mold line above right ear. Jumeau mark has been scrubbed from rear of head.
$900-$1,100

Jumeau Bébé
24" Jumeau Bébé marked "P.11." Special order from Jumeau, with blue paperweight eyes and even bisque. Wearing a French human hair wig with a blue wool antique Mariner's outfit. Hairline behind left ear (no paint or restoration). On a repainted straight-wrist Schmitt body.
$1,800-$1,900

Portrait Jumeau

24" first series portrait Jumeau #4. Amber eyes with an almond eye cut. Restoration to head above eyebrows (forehead); small eye chip repair to the rim of the lower left eye. Body is a Kestner, straight-wrist composition, ball-jointed.

$3,000-$3,500

Poupée

25" French bisque Poupée Jumeau. Blue paperweight eyes, original cork pate and auburn mohair wig. On a leather fashion body wearing antique baby gown and underwear. Hairline crack from left eye going back towards ear and up to rim.

$1,000-$1,200

Long Face

25" "long face" Jumeau. Called a "Triste" Jumeau. Marked on rear of head with number "11" and is on an eight-ball-jointed marked Jumeau body, also with Paris store label, "JEUX & JOUETS." Pale bisque with light mauve shadowing, blue paperweight eyes and sandy blonde mohair wig. Marked size "11" French leather shoes (frail condition) and wearing an aqua checked wool frock with feather stitching and matching aqua hat. Original spring in head, but is loosely strung and has normal minor wear to body joints.

$16,500-$17,500

Jumeau Bébé
26" Jumeau Bébé, marked "12 Jumeau, French Bébé," open mouth, brown stationary eyes, fully jointed Jumeau composition toddler body, wearing orange dress and sunbonnet, leather shoes.

$6,000-$8,000

Portrait Face
26" "portrait face" Jumeau fashion. On a gusseted kid and cloth body (appears several leather fingers have been reattached). Attached ears, blue paperweight eyes, creamy bisque, and painted eyebrows. Dressed in a royal blue leaded silk dress with dark velvet apron, collar puffs and bustle, and gold leaf earrings. Original sandy mohair wig and a silk-lined straw bonnet. Dress is fragile and shows signs of wear and melting in various spots, the dress has not been removed for inspection of body. Head has inherent mold flaw above right ear extending a little over 1/4" from crown and meeting seam line.

$3,300-$3,700

Tete Jumeau
27" Tete Jumeau #12. Blue paperweight eyes and fine bisque. On a fully jointed marked Jumeau body. Wearing an antique white cotton eyelet dress and newer human hair wig. Lacking shoes. Body has normal wear at joints and some repainting throughout.

$3,500-$4,000

K&K Toy Co., founded 1915

This New York firm imported bisque heads from Germany, and supplied cloth and composition bodies to other companies, including George Borgfeldt. Composition bodies were often marked "bisquette" or "fiberoid." While most bisque doll heads marked "K&K" are found on cloth bodies with composition limbs, occasionally one is found on a kid body with bisque arms. (Also see composition.)

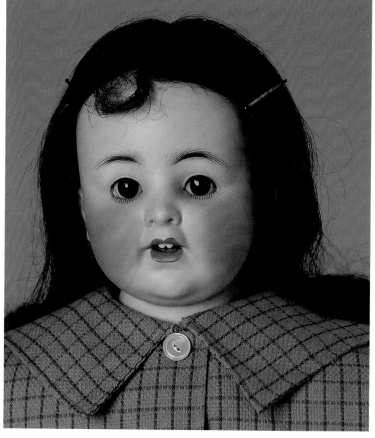

K&K Toddler
23" K&K 60 bisque toddler. Shoulder-head toddler, on a "mama" type body. Brown sleep eyes, long dark human hair wig, original underwear, shoes and socks, and is wearing a plaid overcoat. Body appears to have original finish with very little wear.
$400-$500

Kämmer & Reinhardt, founded 1886

Ernst Kämmer and Franz Reinhardt started their firm in Waltershausen, Thüringia, Germany, designing but not manufacturing doll heads. Simon & Halbig made most of the bisque heads and became part of Kämmer & Reinhardt by 1920.

The "W" found on the forehead of some Kämmer & Reinhardt dolls may refer to the Waltershausen region. Some numbers (starting with 15) found low on the doll's neck indicate sizes in centimeters, not mold numbers.

Kämmer & Reinhardt introduced its K(star)R character dolls on bent-limb baby bodies at the 1909 Munich Exhibit. The firm also made cloth dolls, which today are rarely found.

K(star)R with Trunk
9" K(star)R/Simon & Halbig 21 with trunk. Open-mouth doll with blue sleep eyes, brown mohair wig, on a jointed German composition body with straight wrists. Accompanied by red dome-top trunk with several outfits. Some discoloration to lower arms, some wear at joints.
$1,200-$1,500/set

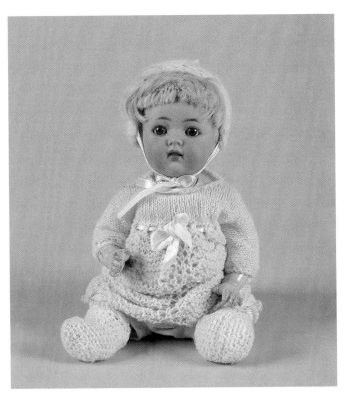

Bisque Boy
10" bisque head baby, marked "K(star)R Simon Halbig 121," open mouth with tongue, blue stationary eyes, composition baby body, wearing a pink knit sweater and cap.

$600-$700

Gretchen
12" K(star)R 114 "Gretchen." Pale blue eyes, on a pink fully jointed composition body. Dressed in a white cotton frock and blonde mohair wig with braids. Composition body has crazing to lower legs and some paint touch up throughout. Bisque has peppering, most noticeable on left cheek. Small white pinprick, also on left cheek.

$750-$850

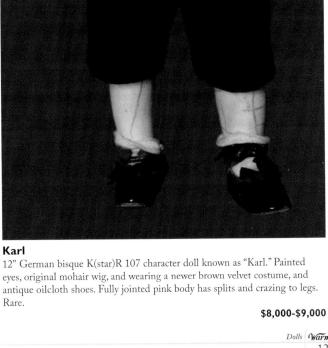

Karl
12" German bisque K(star)R 107 character doll known as "Karl." Painted eyes, original mohair wig, and wearing a newer brown velvet costume, and antique oilcloth shoes. Fully jointed pink body has splits and crazing to legs. Rare.

$8,000-$9,000

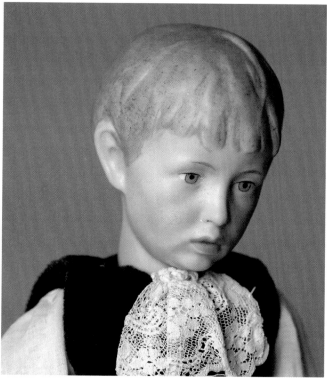

K(star)R
12" German bisque K(star)R 102 with molded hair. Wearing newer velvet costume. Small chip in neck socket. Light dusting to bisque. Fully jointed composition body in good condition. Rare.

$11,000-$12,000

K(star)R
14 1/2" K(star)R Simon & Halbig with blue sleep eyes, open mouth with teeth, fully jointed composition body, wearing a whit eyelet dress.

$600-$800

Character Child
14" German bisque K(star)R 109 character child. With painted eyes, dressed in antique regional boy's costume, replaced blonde human hair wig. On a fully jointed K(star)R body. Cotton dress and hat included. Minor scuffing on tip of nose and upper lip, and small rough patches to left forehead and cheek. Not visible when wig is in place.

$4,500-$5,500

Max

16" K(star)R bisque character 123 known as "Max." Dressed in older clothes. Brown human hair wig and French body. Also included, one book featuring Max and Moritz characters. Two hairlines to back of head. French body has wear on hands and is a replacement.

$2,200-$2,400

Moritz

16" K(star)R bisque character 124 known as "Moritz." Blue "flirty" eyes and original wig. Dressed in felt, with K(star)R body. Also included, one book featuring Max and Moritz characters. Body has a re-glue at ankle, two broken fingers, some crazing, but retains original finish.

$13,500-$14,500

Character Baby

16" German bisque K&R 122 character baby. Brown sleep eyes, wobble tongue, newer human hair wig, on a five-piece, bent-limb baby body. Light scuffing on cheeks and tip of nose. Roughness on forehead. Body has some repaint on hands only.

$350-$400

Bisque Head

16" bisque head, marked "Simon & Halbig, K(star)R 126," open mouth with teeth, blue sleep eyes, jointed composition body, wearing a cream-colored cotton dress.

$700+

Doll and Trunk

17" K(star)R 117N with trunk and wardrobe. Brown flirty glass sleep eyes, on a pink jointed composition K(star)R body (split on lower arm, which has been reglued and touched up). Wearing a provincial outfit with black leather heeled shoes and original black braided mohair wig.

$1,700-$1,800

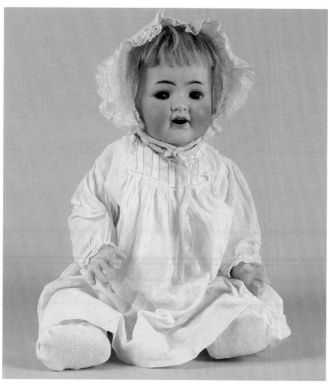

Bisque Head

20" bisque head, marked "K(star)R Simon Halbig 126, Baby Patty," open mouth with teeth, brown sleep eyes, jointed composition baby body, wearing a white cotton baby dress with lace and white lace bonnet.

$750+

Marie

20" bisque head "Marie," marked K(star)R, intaglio eyes, closed mouth, hair is braided around ear, jointed composition body, wearing a pink checked dress.

$3,000+

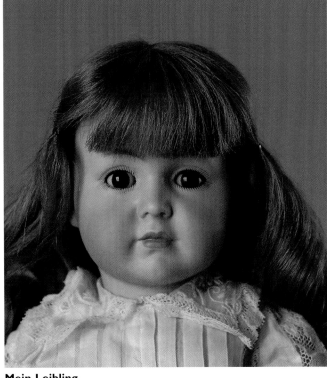

Bisque Head
21" bisque head, marked "156 K(star)R Simon Halbig 403," brown stationary eyes, open mouth with teeth, jointed composition toddler body (walking doll), brown wig, wearing a white embroidered cotton dress.
$1,500+

Mein Leibling
22" K(star)R 117 "Mein Leibling." Wearing an antique white cotton dress, brown boots, and a replacement brown human hair wig. Amber sleep eyes, clean bisque, on composition ball-jointed body. Very fine condition.
$4,000-$4,500

Bisque Head
24" bisque head K(star)R Simon & Halbig 403, open mouth with teeth, blue stationary eyes, fully jointed composition body, redressed for display.
$700-$800

Character Baby
25" K(star)R Simon & Halbig 126 character baby, open mouth with teeth, blonde wig, blue flirty sleep eyes, composition jointed baby body, dressed in a tan cotton suit with red trim (pictured in old wicker stroller).
$1,200-$1,300

Bisque Head
30" K(star)R Simon & Halbig bisque head, blue stationary eyes, open mouth with teeth, pierced ears, all jointed composition body, in a rose-colored dress, white pinafore, leather shoes.
$1,700+

J. D. Kestner, after 1860

Though the company was founded in 1816 in Waltershausen, Germany, Kestner bisque dolls were introduced following the acquisition of a porcelain factory in 1860. Kestner produced complete dolls, and also supplied doll heads to other manufacturers.

The firm used various markings, including its name, initials, mold numbers, and a series of letters. "Excelsior" was a trade name of Kestner dolls distributed in the United States. The bisque-head dolls may be found with various body types.

Bisque Girl
7" all bisque girl, moveable arms and legs, marked "150-1 Kestner," open mouth, sleep eyes, molded shoes and socks, wearing a cream-colored ecru net dress.

$700+

Bisque Head
8" bisque head, marked "Germany 12/0 Kestner," brown eyes, blonde wig, open mouth with teeth, jointed composition body, painted legs and shoes, wearing a plaid dress, white apron and hat.

$400+

Bisque Dome Head
10" bisque dome head, marked "JDK, Made in Germany, Kestner," open/closed mouth, blue stationary eyes, composition body, wearing a white dotted Swiss-style dress.

$450+

Character Baby
12" bisque dome head character baby, marked "Made in Germany JDK," blue sleep eyes, fur hair, open mouth with teeth, composition baby body, wearing a teal velvet outfit.
$400-$450

German Child
12 1/2" German bisque Kestner 143 child. With brown sleep eyes, open mouth with two upper teeth, and fully jointed Kestner body. Brown mohair wig with coiled braids, in antique oriental costume. Original body finish. Overall excellent condition.
$550-$600

Bisque Head
13" bisque head, marked "Made in Germany 143 Kestner," brown wig, open mouth with teeth, brown stationary eyes, jointed body, wearing a white embroidered cotton dress.
$700+

Bisque Swivel Head
15" bisque swivel head on bisque shoulder plate ("Bru face"), marked "54/7 Kestner," brown stationary eyes, open mouth with teeth, kid body, wearing a white dress with lace, pink roses and ribbons, and straw hat.
$1,400-$1,600

Bisque Shoulder Head
17" bisque shoulder head, marked "154 DEP Made in Germany Kestner," brown sleep eyes, open mouth with teeth, kid body, bisque lower arms, wearing a blue crocheted dress and star hat.
$375-$450

Bisque Dome Head
17" bisque dome head, marked "R-10 Kestner," open mouth with teeth, brown stationary eyes, painted comb-streaked hair, composition baby body, wearing a white cotton baby dress.

$1,000+

Turned Shoulder Head
18" bisque turned shoulder head Kestner, marked "T Germany," excellent coloring, brown paperweight eyes, open/closed mouth, kid body, wearing a cream-colored dress, black stockings, and cream-colored leather boots.

$1,000+

Turned Shoulder Head
18" bisque turned shoulder head, marked "L. Kestner," closed mouth, blue threaded eyes, old leather body including hands, dressed in ecru lace and pink crocheted hat (head has been professionally repaired).

As is, $500; if perfect, $1,000+

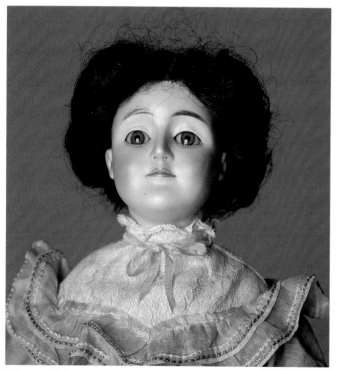

Gibson Girl
20" German bisque Kestner, known as "Gibson Girl," marked 172. Blue sleep eyes, on a replaced leather body with composition lower limbs. Human hair wig and a green silk two-piece walking suit. Some small peppering to chin and side of nose. One or more hairlines to back of head with paint touchup.

$400-$500

Character Baby
20" German bisque Kestner character baby. Molded hair and brown sleep eyes. Open mouth with wobble tongue and two teeth. On a bent limb Kestner baby body and dressed in antique baby clothes. Overall light dusting to bisque. Body is in excellent original condition. Clothes are shredding.

$700-$800

Kestner Shoulder Head
21" Kestner shoulder head marked "154." Blue sleep eyes, open mouth with teeth, kid body, wearing an orange dress with ecru lace, brown lace stockings, leather shoes.

$500+

German Boy
22" German bisque JDK 214 boy. Black tuxedo with antique boots, original sandy blonde mohair wig and green felt hat. Brown sleep-eyes, on a jointed composition body marked "Heinrich Handwerck." Repaired neck, small eye chip on upper lid, body not original.

$175-$225

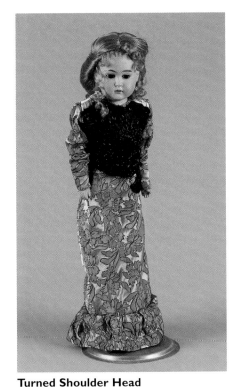

Turned Shoulder Head
22" Kestner bisque turned shoulder head, brown stationary eyes, open mouth with teeth, kid body dressed in black beaded top over blue satin (back shoulder plate repaired).

As is, $250; if perfect, $550+

Shoulder Head
Left, 22" Kestner bisque shoulder head, marked "DEP 10154 Made in Germany," open mouth with teeth, brown stationary eyes, mint kid body, wearing a maroon silk dress and bonnet.

$700+

Right, 24" bisque head, marked with an "H" containing a small "K" in the upper section and a 4 in the lower section, open mouth with teeth, blue stationary eyes, jointed composition body, wearing a pink striped satin dress.

$500+

Character Baby
23" Kestner character baby, blonde hair (firing flaw on back of bisque head), blue sleep eyes, open mouth with teeth, fully jointed composition body, wearing a cream-colored dress and bonnet.
$500-$700

Bisque Dome Head
24" Kestner bisque dome head, marked "JDK Made in Germany," blue sleep eyes, fully jointed composition body, wearing a white cotton baby dress and bonnet.
$1,200-$1,400

Kid Body
24" Kestner 167 on kid body. Swivel neck with bisque shoulder plate. Brown sleep eyes, replaced human hair wig, and even complexion. Wearing a two-piece striped cotton lady's dress. Four fingers broken on right hand, head has hairline on back of neck.
$175-$225

Closed-Mouthed
24" closed-mouthed Kestner. Marked "15" on back of head, brown glass sleep eyes, and pale bisque. On an early chunky straight-wrist Kestner body. Blonde mohair wig, antique leather shoes and undergarments, and an aqua dress with black velvet trim with matching tam. Some dustiness to the outside of right cheek.
$2,000-$3,000

Shoulder Head

25" bisque shoulder head, marked "Made in Germany, 166 Kestner," open mouth with teeth, blue sleep eyes, kid body with sewed-on boot, wearing white dress with maroon belt.

$600+

Shoulder Head

26" Kestner shoulder head, marked with a crown and "N," brown stationary eyes, closed mouth, deep shoulder chest, unusual leather body, wearing a white blouse, black velvet skirt with elaborate trim.

$1,000+

Turned Shoulder Head

26" Kestner turned shoulder head. Brown sleep eyes and pale bisque. On a cloth body with bisque lower arms, wearing child's peach wool dress trimmed with blue braid, and children's boots with wooden heels. Wig is a blonde human hair replacement. Small pepper flake on chin. Lower legs are recovered.

$350-$400

Shoulder Head

29" Kestner bisque shoulder head, marked "DEP 154-13 Made in Germany," with a crown on chest, tagged "corkstuffed" on chest, blue sleep eyes, open mouth with teeth, curly blonde mohair wig, excellent kid body, wearing a cream-colored silk gown.

$700-$800

Kestner

30" bisque-head Kestner, marked "Germany," brown stationary eyes, open mouth with teeth, brown curly wig, (pull mark behind ear), fully jointed composition body, wearing white dress with blue beads.

$800+

Kestner

30" bisque-head Kestner, marked "DEP-154 N," open mouth with teeth, brown sleep eyes, kid leather body, composition arms and hands, wearing an elaborate ecru dress and cap, leather shoes.

$900-$1,200

Turned Shoulder Head

30" Kestner bisque turned shoulder head, deep chest (front of chest cracked and repaired), brown stationary eyes, open mouth with teeth, kid body, wearing a white cotton eyelet dress.

As is, $700; if perfect, $1,000+

Kley & Hahn, founded 1902

Founded in Ohrdruf, Thüringia, Germany, by Albert Kley and Paul Hahn, the firm's specialty was making character dolls for the American market.

Several porcelain factories contributed to the Kley & Hahn inventory, including Bahr & Pröschild, Hertel, Schwab & Co., and Kestner.

Walküre
29" German bisque Kley & Hahn "Walküre." Sandy blonde mohair wig, brown sleep eyes, on a fully jointed chunky German composition body, wearing an antique white windowpane and crochet child's dress. One finger reglued, minor wear to joints. Head has crack from crown, down between eyes to left brow.

$150-$200

Walküre
30" bisque Kley & Hahn "Walküre," marked "7 Germany Walküre," stationary threaded blue-gray eyes, open mouth with teeth, wearing a blue embroidered dress, old high-button shoes (body in fair condition, repaired crack behind head).
As is, $1,000+; without crack, $3,000+

Gebrüder Kuhnlenz, founded 1884

The firm was established by three brothers — Julius, Cuno, and Bruno — in Kronach, Bavaria.

Bisque Head
8" bisque head, marked "G50K" in a sunburst and "44-17," blue stationary eyes, open mouth with teeth, composition body with hands made to hold a flag (sometimes shown with bisque animal on string), wearing a navy suit and hat.
$300+

Shoulder-Head Lady
20" German bisque G.K. 38-28 shoulder-head lady. Blue paperweight eyes, pierced ears, and human hair wig. Solid dome head, kid body with bisque lower arms. Black scratch on right cheek, tiny pits to finish of right eye. Body has some patching at gussets.
$250-$300

Porcelain Dolls

A. Lanternier et Cie, founded 1855

This French firm located in Limoges began making doll heads in 1915. The quality of their work ranges from very good to coarse and grainy.

A. G. Limbach, mid-19th century

The firm that became A.G. Limbach was started by Gotthelf Greiner, near Alsbach, Thüringia, Germany. The Sonneberg, Germany, Museum has identified a china shoulder-head doll dating from 1850 as having been made by Limbach. Production of bisque doll heads was temporarily discontinued in 1899, resuming in 1919.

Character Boy
20" French bisque character boy marked A-7. Possibly Lanternier, circa 1920. Blue paperweight eyes and open/closed mouth with two teeth and molded tongue. Blond mohair wig, on a French jointed composition body and redressed in Buster Brown costume. Small pepper marks on face, and hands are repainted. Some discoloration under right eye.
$1,000-$1,300

German Bisque
14" German bisque doll marked with a cloverleaf on back of head. Brown paperweight eyes. Floral print cotton dress trimmed in red satin, original brimmed hat with feather on top, gauze underwear, black knit socks and oilcloth shoes. On a fully jointed straight-wrist body. Original short sandy blonde mohair wig. Body has original finish with very little wear.
$500-$700

Limbach Girl
22" German bisque Limbach girl is marked with cloverleaf on the back of head and a "12." Blue paperweight eyes, open mouth with two square-cut teeth. On a straight-wrist fully jointed composition body. Human hair wig is a newer replacement, and new dress and hat are made in the French manner. Brown oilcloth shoes and white cotton underwear. Composition body has been repainted. Some peppering to right brow and tip of nose.
$550-$650

Armand Marseille, 1885 to 1930

Located in Sonneberg and Köppelsdorf, Thüringia, Germany, Armand Marseille was one of the largest suppliers of bisque doll heads in the world, reportedly producing a thousand heads a day. Companies using Armand Marseille heads include Amberg, Arranbee, C. M. Bergmann, Borgfeldt, Butler Bros., Cuno & Otto Dressel, Eckart, Edelmann, Otto Gans, Goldberger, Hitz, Jacobs & Kassler, Illfelder, E. Maar, Montgomery Ward, Emil Pfeiffer, Peter Scherf, Seyfarth & Reinhardt, Siegel Cooper, E.U. Steiner, Wagner & Wetzsche, Wislizenus, and Louis Wolf & Co.

Dome-Head Babies
8" bisque dome-head babies, marked "AM Germany 1440K," blue sleep eyes, closed mouths, wearing bunting.
$275+ each

Googly
9" German bisque A.M. 200 Googly. Five-piece body with side-glancing blue eyes. Human hair wig with newer clothes. Overall excellent, body somewhat dirty but retains original paint.
$1,750-$2,000

Jointed Body
9 1/2" all bisque, jointed body, marked "Armand Marseilles Germany 390," open mouth with teeth, sleep eyes, wearing a cream-colored dress and bonnet.
$200+

Bisque Head

11" bisque head, marked "Armand Marseilles 390 A5/0M," brown sleep eyes, open mouth with teeth, blonde wig, jointed composition body, wearing a cream-colored cotton and lace dress.

$200+

Bisque Head

11" bisque head, marked "390 AM," sleep eyes, open mouth with teeth, composition body, wearing a traditional Dutch costume and wooden shoes, all of which are original.

$200-$250

Bisque Head

11" bisque head, marked "AM 3/1 DEP," brown stationary eyes, open mouth with teeth, composition toddler body, dark brown curly wig, wearing an old satin dress with blue ribbons.

$250-$300

Bisque Dome Head

12" bisque dome head (8" circumference) baby, marked "Germany 371 AM," blue stationary eyes, closed mouth, cloth body, celluloid hands, wearing a long white dress.

$450-$500

Scowling Indian
11" bisque head (Scowling Indian), marked "Armand Marseilles," dark glass eyes, open mouth with teeth, cardboard papier-mâché body marked "4-0," stick-type limbs, wearing a printed costume.

$150+

1894 Girl
12" German bisque A.M. 1894 girl, dressed in patriotic outfit representing "Miss Columbia." Retains original wig and shoes. Open mouth and four teeth, and fully jointed composition body. Some discoloration to right side of forehead, light scuffing on the arms, some wear and touch-up to knee joints. Fabric is weak on costume with overall soiling.

$200-$300

Character Baby
12" bisque head character baby, marked "AM 985," blue stationary eyes, open mouth with teeth, jointed baby body, wearing a white cotton dress.

$325-$375

Character Baby
12" bisque head character baby, marked "Armand Marseilles, Germany," blue sleep eyes, open mouth with teeth, jointed baby body, wearing a white cotton dress with pink ribbon.

$350+

Topsy-Turvy
12" bisque shoulder head topsy-turvy doll, marked "AM" on white head, paperweight eyes, open mouth with teeth, composition hands, cotton body stuffed with excelsior; black head is painted papier-mâché, black mohair wig, brown glass eyes, painted mouth, composition hands.

$500+

Scowling Indian

12 1/2" bisque head (Scowling Indian), marked "4/0 Armand Marseilles," open mouth with teeth, brown stationary eyes, composition body, wearing white leather outfit, beaded and fringed.

$250+

Bisque Head

13" bisque head, marked "Made in Germany, Armand Marseilles, 390," brown sleep eyes, open mouth with teeth, stick body, wearing blue satin dress with white lace.

$200-$250

Fany

13" A.M. Fany #231. Blue glass sleep eyes, on straight wrist, short chunky body. Wearing a yellow cotton print dress and blonde mohair wig. Lacking shoes. Repainting to lower arms and thighs. Eye chip on doll's lower left rim by nose.

$1,500-$2,000

Bisque Head

13" bisque head, marked "Made in Germany 390 A3/0M," open mouth with teeth, blue stationary eyes, old stick body, black wig, wearing a white satin dress.

$200-$250

Bisque Head
14" bisque head, marked "Armand Marseilles, Germany 390," blue stationary eyes, open mouth with teeth, jointed composition body, wearing a cream-colored satin dress with pearls.

$200-$250

Googly
13 1/2" German bisque A.M. 253 Googly. White eyelet and cloth shoes. Original blonde mohair wig and side-glancing brown sleep eyes. Minor wear.

$3,500-$4,000

Flapper Lady
14" A.M. 401 flapper lady. With blue sleep eyes and brown mohair wig. Original underwear, stockings and shoes, and a knit pink and white cotton dress with matching hat. Composition flapper style body. Lacking some fingertips on both hands, ball joints have paint chipping.

$1,400-$1,800

Bisque Head
14" bisque head, marked "Ottogans, Germany 975 A 2 M," open mouth with teeth, blonde wig, brown sleep eyes, composition body, wearing a white cotton dress with ruffles.

$500+

Bisque Dome Head

Left, 14" bisque dome head baby, marked "AM Germany 341-13," baby open/close eyes, closed mouth, cloth body, celluloid hands, wearing a white cotton dress and sweater.

$500+

Right, 12" bisque dome head, marked "Baby Phyllis, Made in Germany," blue sleep eyes, closed mouth, cloth body, composition hands, wearing a white cotton dress.

$400-$450

Bisque Baby

14 1/2" German bisque A.M. GB 329 baby. Blue-gray sleep eyes, original blonde mohair wig, which has never been removed. Five-piece baby body has original pink finish, wearing a pink checked romper and sweater set. Open mouth with two lower teeth. Two missing fingers on left hand, light wear to the finish on both hands, and chipping on toes. Left arm needs to be restrung.

$250-$300

Bisque Head

14 1/2" bisque head, marked "Made in Germany AM," brown stationary eyes, open mouth with teeth, blonde wig, jointed body, wearing a cream colored snowsuit and skates.

$250+

Bisque Head

14 1/2" bisque head, marked "Armand Marseilles, Germany 370 A 3/0 M," brown sleep eyes, open mouth with two teeth, new fully jointed body, wearing a wool snowsuit with fur trim.

$150+

Character Baby

15" bisque head character baby, marked "Germany 971 A #4 M DRGM," brown stationary eyes, open mouth with teeth, jointed composition baby body, wearing an off-white dotted cotton dress and bonnet with blue ribbon.

$400+

Bisque Head

15" bisque head, marked "Made in Germany 390 AM," brown stationary eyes, open mouth with teeth, fully jointed composition toddler body, wearing a blue cotton dress.

$250+

Shoulder Head

15" bisque shoulder head, marked "1894 AM 3/0 X, DEP," open mouth with teeth, brown stationary eyes, kid body, wearing a blue dress with white lace trim.

$375-$425

Floradora Girl

16" German bisque A.M. Floradora girl. Brown sleep eyes, original mohair wig. On a jointed kid body with cloth lower legs and stone bisque lower arms. Open mouth with four molded teeth. Redressed in a red plaid cotton dress. Excellent condition.

$100-$150

Bisque Head

16" bisque head, marked "1894 AM 8 DEP," brown stationary eyes, open mouth with teeth, light complexion, blonde wig, composition body, wearing a yellow dress.

$300-$350

Shoulder Head

17" bisque shoulder head, marked "Germany 370 A5/0M Armand Marseilles," blue stationary eyes, open mouth with teeth, excellent kid body, wearing a pink dress and hat.

$200+

Armand Marseilles

18" Armand Marseilles, marked "AM 1894 2 DEP," brown stationary eyes, open mouth with teeth, jointed composition body, wearing a white cotton and crocheted dress.

$500+

Bisque Head

18" bisque head, marked "AM 390 Germany," brown sleep eyes, open mouth with teeth, blonde wig, jointed composition body, wearing a wine-colored satin dress, black stockings, and leather shoes.

$300-$350

Painted Bisque

19" painted bisque, marked "AM," blue sleep eyes, open mouth with teeth, molded braided hair over ears, jointed composition body, wearing a navy skirt and embroidered vest and blouse, and black and white leather shoes.

$350+

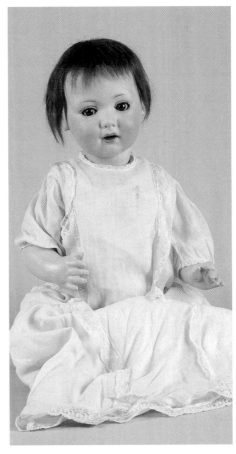

Shoulder Head
19" bisque shoulder head, marked "370 AM 1/2 DEP Armand Marseilles," dark wig, blue sleep eyes (chip under one eye), open mouth with teeth, "kidolene" body, wearing a green lace dress and hat, leather shoes.
As is, $150-$200; if perfect, $300-$350

Character Baby
21" bisque head character baby, marked "Germany G 37 B, DRGM 259 A 9 M," blue sleep eyes, open mouth with teeth, jointed composition body, wearing a long white baby dress.
$1,350+

Bisque Head
22" bisque head, marked "390 BRGM 246 A7M, Bergmann and Armand Marseilles," blue stationary eyes, open mouth with teeth, fully jointed body, wearing an ecru net embroidered dress.
$500-$600

Shoulder Head
22" Armand Marseilles shoulder head, marked "Floradora AM Made in Germany," blue stationary eyes, open mouth with teeth, brown hair, kid body, wearing an elaborate dress and hat.
$375+

Porcelain Dolls

Shoulder Head
22" Armand Marseilles shoulder head, marked "370 AM 2 DEP Armand Marseilles – Made in Germany," blue stationary eyes, open mouth with teeth, kid body, wearing a cream-colored dress with lace and pink flowers, leather boots.

$350+

Shoulder Head
22" bisque shoulder head, marked "AM 370," blue stationary eyes, open mouth with teeth, brown wig, jointed kid body, wearing two-piece tangerine-pink dress with ecru lace and matching hat.

$350+

Shoulder Head
22" bisque shoulder head, marked "AM 370 Germany," blue sleep eyes, long brown curls, open mouth with teeth, kid body, wearing a cotton dress with insertion lace.

$325-$375

Bisque Head
24" bisque head, marked "Queen Louise, Made in Germany," blue threaded stationary eyes, open mouth with teeth, jointed composition body, wearing an old dress of dark gold silk, 1920s style, with red trim and olive green sateen.

$450-$500

Bisque Head
24" bisque head Armand Marseilles, marked "390 DRGM 246/1 390H A 7 1/2 M," blue stationary eyes, fully jointed body, dressed in historical-style costume for display.

$400+

Bisque Head
24" bisque head, marked "390 Armand Marseilles," brown sleep eyes, open mouth with teeth, blonde wig, jointed composition body, wearing a white cotton embroidered dress.

$400-$450

Shoulder Head
24" bisque shoulder head, marked "Germany 370 A3M Armand Marseilles," blue sleep eyes, open mouth with teeth, blonde wig, kid body, wearing a checked dress with red satin trim, leather shoes stitched on body.

$325-$375

Shoulder Head
25" bisque shoulder head, marked "AM 51/2 DEP 390 Made in Germany," open mouth with teeth, blue stationary eyes, kid body, wearing a white cotton dress.

$500+

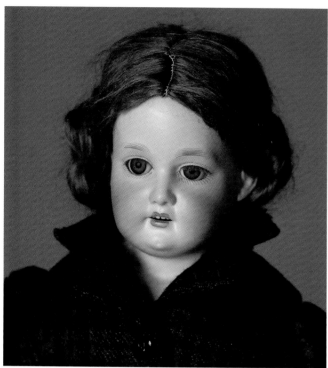

Shoulder Head

25" A.M. 370. Shoulder head, on a simulated kid body with cloth upper arms and lower bisque arms. Blue sleep eyes and mohair wig, dressed in a wool lady's jacket and skirt. Body has normal soiling and wear, tape at the shoulder plate, and two broken fingers.

$175-$225

Bisque Head

25" bisque head, marked "DRGM 377439 Made in Germany A 10 M 390," fur eyebrows, brown stationary eyes (hairline cracks on both sides of head under wig), fully jointed body, wearing a blue cotton dress.

As is, $300+; if perfect $450+

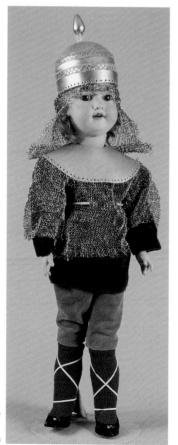

Bisque Head

6" bisque head, marked "AM DRGM," sleep eyes, open mouth with teeth, jointed body, redressed for historical display.

$500-$600

Bisque Head

27" bisque head, marked "Armand Marseilles 390 Germany A9M," blue stationary eyes, open mouth with teeth, brown wig, jointed composition body, wearing a cream-colored lace dress, white stockings and leather shoes.

$500-$600

Armand Marseilles
29" Armand Marseilles, marked "Made in Germany
– Armand Marseilles – 390 DRGM 246/A11M," brown
stationary eyes, long brown hair, fully jointed composition
body, burgundy velvet dress with lace trim.

$550-$650

Bisque Head
40" bisque head, marked "AM," brown stationary eyes,
open mouth with teeth, replaced papier-mâché body parts,
wearing a white girl's dress and leather shoes.

$2,000+

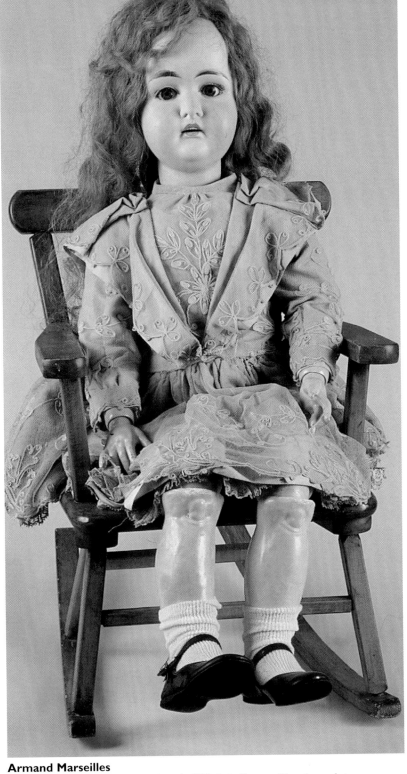

Armand Marseilles
35" Armand Marseilles, bisque head, marked "Made in Germany," long brown hair, open
mouth with teeth, stationary blue eyes, fully jointed body in good condition, wearing blue-gray
net-lace dress (face repaired).

As is, $500; if perfect, $1,000+

Mascotte Bébé

19" French bisque Mascotte Bébé. Closed mouth with blue paperweight eyes on a fully jointed composition body marked "BÉBÉ MASCOTTE." Retains some underwear and socks. Wig is a French human hair replacement. Body is in fine original condition with some scuffs and dirt to torso.

$3,500-$4,000

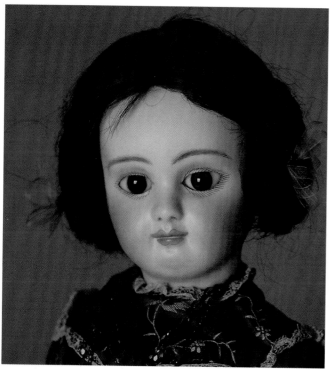

Bébé Mothereau

22" Bébé Mothereau. Marked on rear of head "B. 9 M." Brown threaded paperweight eyes, on a jointed French body. Wearing an embroidered brown Porcelain Bébé dress, human hair wig with braids covering each ear, and antique leather shoes. Couple black specks on face.

$8,000-$9,000

Alexandre Mothereau, 1880 to 1895

Solid information about Alexandre Celestin Triburee Mothereau is scarce. The French firm produced Bébé Mothereau for only about 15 years.

The bodies have turned-wooden upper limbs and rounded-joint lower limbs, with metal brackets to accept elastic stringing. They have long and thin torsos, and small hands and feet.

Bébé Mothereau

28" Bébé Mothereau. With light brown threaded paperweight eyes with mauve eye shadowing. Original skin wig. Possibly original red cotton dress with black piping and marked French shoes. Rear of head is marked "B. 10 M." On French straight-wrist composition body. Overall condition is very fine, skin wig has not been removed. Rare.

$15,000-$16,000

Petit & Dumontier, 1878 to 1890

Founded by Frederic Petit and Andre Dumontier, with some heads made by Francois Gaultier.

Petit & Dumontier Bébé

17" French P. 1. D. Petit & Dumontier Bébé. On a jointed composition body (incorrect) with blue paperweight eyes, dressed in white cotton dress with blue highlighting. Although head has had restoration, the facial details have not been affected.

$1,800-$2,200

Petit & Dumontier Bébé

18" French P. 2. D. Petit & Dumontier Bébé (circa 1880s) with dark brown paperweight eyes and some mauve eye shadowing. Pale bisque on a fully jointed composition body with metal hands. Dressed in an antique child's white cotton dress. Wearing antique shoes and socks. Sandy blonde human hair wig with curls. Overall condition is very fine with normal wear to body at joints. Some paint loss to metal hands. Rare.

$11,500-$12,500

P.5 D. Bébé

26" French P. 5 D. Petit & Dumontier Bébé with bulbous blue paperweight eyes, pale bisque, on the proper composition ball-jointed composition body with metal hands. Wearing antique velvet dress with shoulder cuffs and lace trim at shoulders (majority of velvet has dissipated) and white two-strap shoes. Replacement auburn human hair wig. Wear and flaking to lower arms and metal hands.

$9,000-$11,000

P.5 D.

26" French P. 5 D. Large almond-eye cut and blue paperweight eyes. On a jointed French style body (not correct), wearing a sea-foam green antique dress, replaced human hair wig and straw bonnet. Body has been repainted, nose has slight rub.

$5,500-$6,000

Pintel & Godchaux, 1887 to 1899

Based in Montreuil-sous-Bois, France, Pintel & Godchaux registered the trade name "Bébé Charmat" in 1892. They also received a patent for a body with a diagonal hip joint.

Pintel & Godchaux Bébé
24" French Pintel & Godchaux Bébé. Marked "P 11 G" on rear of head. Blue paperweight eyes, on a composition and wood French ball-jointed body, wearing a replica French outfit. Bisque has a few pimples: one on eyebrow and a couple on the cheek.

$1,900-$2,300

Pintel & Godchaux Bébé
14" French bisque P.G. Bébé. Attributed to Pintel & Godchaux, on a fully jointed wood and composition body. Blue paperweight eyes with even bisque. Dressed in antique underwear and shoes with a replacement blonde human hair wig. Comes with newer French-style costume. Overall very good to excellent.

$1,500-$2,000

Rabery & Delphieu, 1856 to 1899

A Paris manufacturer focusing on doll bodies, the company became part of the Societe Française de Fabrication des Bébés et Jouets in 1899. In the last quarter of the 19th century, Francois Gaultier supplied bisque heads and arms for Rabery & Delphieu Bébés. These were made using both pressed and poured bisque methods.

Rabery & Delphieu
15" Rabery & Delphieu. Brown paperweight eyes and uniform bisque. Marked "R 2/O D." On a jointed French composition body and wearing original factory chemise, with original French blonde mohair wig (sparse). Small damage to side of torso, probably where doll stand was placed on doll.

$1,400-$1,600

Theodor Recknagel, after 1893

Recknagel's porcelain factory in Alexandrienthal, Thüringia, Germany, was founded in 1886, but there is no evidence of doll production before 1893, when he registered two tinted Mulatto doll heads.

Bisque Heads

Left, 9 1/2" bisque shoulder head, marked "1670," open mouth with teeth, black glass eyes, fabric legs, old white cotton dress with lace.

$200+

Right, 6 1/2" bisque head girl, marked "1909 DEP R 0/0 A, Recknagel of Germany," papier-mâché body (stamped "I can close my eyes – Made in Germany"), blonde mohair wig, blue sleep eyes, open mouth with teeth, wearing a white cotton dress.

$200+

Mme. Rohmer, 1857 to 1880

Marie Antoinette Leontine Rohmer of Paris produced dolls in both china and bisque. She obtained several patents for improvements to doll bodies. The first, for articulated kid body joints, was followed by a patent for gutta percha or rubber doll arms. Another patent was for a new type of doll's head with a cord running through it into the body and out riveted holes in the front of the torso. This allowed turning of the head in any direction and also secured the head to the body.

Rohmer Fashion

18" Rohmer fashion. "Cup and saucer" neck on a marked kid body. Bisque arms attached to the leather upper, which swivel at the shoulder. Pale bisque, blue eyes. Wearing a striped blue and white wool outfit, black leather boots and a cotton blouse with blue piping, a (possibly original) sandy blonde human hair wig, and a felt pillbox hat with velvet leaf attachments. Outfit has some moth damage.

$3,500-$4,000

Bruno Schmidt, founded 1900

Located in Waltershausen, Germany, records indicate that Bruno Schmidt's character bisque heads were purchased exclusively from Bähr & Pröschild, which Bruno Schmidt eventually acquired.

Schmitt et Fils, 1863 to 1891

This French firm was located at Nogent-sur-Marne, Seine, and Paris.

Schmitt et Fils Bébés usually are made using pressed, rather than poured, bisque. Wax and wax-over papier-mâché examples also have been found. They are typically marked "SCH" with crossed hammers within a shield. (Also see papier-mâché and wax.)

Wendy
11" German bisque Bruno Schmidt 537 character known as "Wendy." Rare petite version of this doll. Original blonde mohair wig. Antique, possibly original clothes. Antique leather shoes marked with a "2." Light pepper on cheek. Light wear to body, one fingertip is missing.

$7,000-$8,000

Schmitt Bébé
14" French Schmitt Bébé. Marked with the Schmitt shield on rear of head and "0" below, threaded blue paperweight eyes, pale bisque, on a straight-wrist, jointed Schmitt (marked) composition body. Wearing a white cotton coat with scarf and muff, a human hair wig, and a pink-feathered hat. Hairline from right eyebrow to top of crown, not readily visible.

$2,000-$2,500

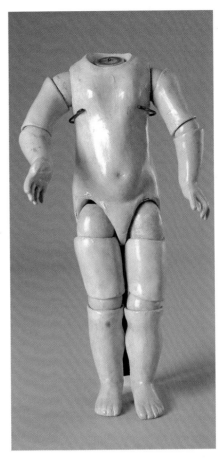

Schmitt Body
17" marked Schmitt body. This 8-ball jointed composition body with straight wrists is in good condition with overpaint and varnish.
$200-$300

Schmitt Bébé
15" Schmitt Bébé. Threaded blue eyes, pale bisque, fully jointed body marked Schmitt. Wearing antique shoes, underwear, blonde mohair wig, and French skirt and jacket with matching hat. Marked on the rear of head with the Schmitt shield and a "0" below, original composition pate is also marked with shield and a "0." Composition body has normal wear at joints although torso shows crazing to composition. A few minor wig chips to side and rear of head. Small pepper mark on doll's left cheek.
$10,000-$13,000

Schmitt Bébé
24" Schmitt Bébé. Blue paperweight. Wearing an antique white cotton dress with lace trim, lace bonnet, and sandy blonde mohair wig. On a marked Schmitt body. White pinprick flake on lower cheek and a hairline extends toward chin continuing up towards nose.
$4,000-$5,000

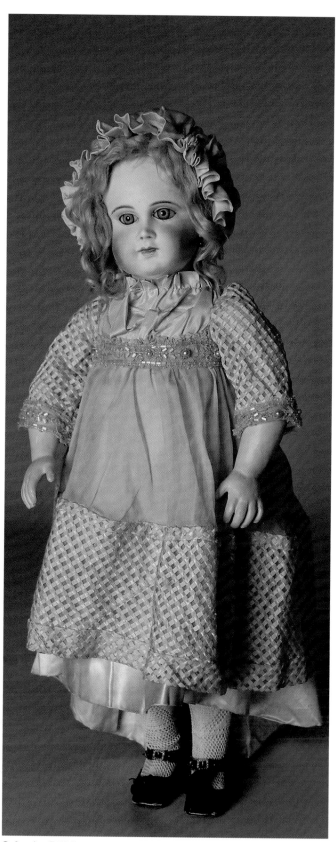

Schmitt Bébé
24" Schmitt Bébé. Brown paperweight eyes with mauve eye shadowing. On a marked Schmitt body. Wearing an antique maroon Bébé dress, and a blonde mohair wig (replaced) and a velvet hat. Minor scuffs to doll's left cheek.

$10,000-$13,000

Schmitt Bébé
25" Schmitt Bébé. Pale bisque, blue threaded paperweight eyes with mauve eye-shadowing. Wearing an antique silk cream dress with a silk ribbon trim throughout and a blonde mohair wig. On a Schmitt body (repainted). One brown pinprick speck between eyebrows.

$11,000-$13,000

Schoenau & Hoffmeister, 1901 to 1953

Located in Burggrub, Bayern, Germany, the factory produced bisque doll heads in both the shoulder-head and socket-head types. They are best remembered for the 1929 Princess Elizabeth Doll.

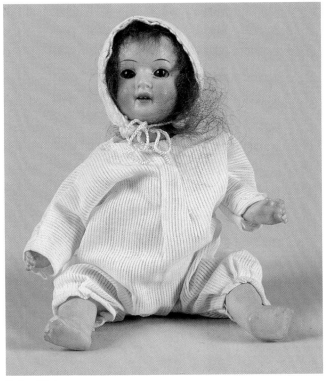

Baby Girl
7 1/2" bisque head baby girl, marked "S*H Hanna 12 1/2 Schoenau & Hoffmeister of Bavaria, Germany," excellent composition jointed body, brown sleep eyes, open mouth with teeth, wearing a white romper.
$500+

Bisque Head
13" bisque head, marked "S*H PB (in star), Schoenman & Porzellanfabrik Burggrub," blue stationary eyes, open mouth with teeth, stick body, wearing a cream-colored dress with pearls.
$200 to $250

Bisque Head
20" bisque head, marked "BP 5859 Germany," blue threaded sleep eyes, open mouth with teeth, jointed composition baby body, wearing a maroon velvet dress and hat with lace.
$500+

Bisque Head
25" bisque head, marked "S*H 1909 Schoenman & Porzellanfabrik Burggrub," open mouth with teeth, brown sleep eyes, composition body, wearing a yellow silk dress.
$500+

Bisque Head
25" bisque head, marked "5500 S*H PB (in star), DEP, Schoenman & Porzellanfabrik Burggrub," blonde wig, pierced ears, brown sleep eyes, jointed composition body, Gibson Girl dress with black bow.
$500-$550

German Child

29" German bisque Schoenau Hoffmeister 5800 child. Brown sleep eyes and original silk lashes. On a fully jointed German composition body, wearing a scarlet sailor suit and red oilcloth shoes. Brown human hair wig and black velvet cap. Body has repair to fingers and repaint to hands and feet, and minute flake to corner of right eye.

$300-$400

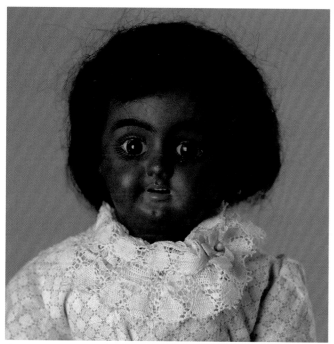

German Child

11 1/2" German brown bisque Simon and Halbig 739 child. Original chocolate brown fully jointed composition body. Brown set eyes and open mouth with four teeth. Newly dressed in blue and white cotton with new shoes, but still retains original black mohair wig, which has never been removed. Wear at neck socket where there appears to be some re-gluing to shoulder seams.

$650-$750

Simon & Halbig, after 1860

Located in Graefenhain and Hildburghausen, near Ohrdruf, Thüringia, Germany, the company made tinted and untinted bisque shoulder heads. Varieties include solid dome, open pate or Belton-Type; molded and painted hair or wigged; painted, stationary, sleep paperweight or flirty eyes; open, closed, or open/closed mouths; and pierced or un-pierced ears.

Black Character

14" black S&H 1368 character. With open mouth, dressed in ethnic costume on a jointed French composition body. Wearing original nappy hair wig, with set light brown paperweight eyes. Antique clothing and shoes. Body overall is fine with minor wear to fingertips and at joints.

$3,500-$4,000

Flapper Lady
14" Simon & Halbig 1469 flapper lady. Gray-blue eyes, flawless bisque, original bobbed blonde mohair wig. Costumed in 1920s style gauze wedding dress and net veil. White leather replacement slippers, long silk stockings, and a bouquet of cloth flowers. Minute flaking at neck socket and some fine crazing to upper legs.
$2,900-$3,300

Oriental
15" Simon & Halbig 1329 oriental. Even skin coloring, original black mohair wig, and costumed in oriental fabrics. On a jointed German composition body with proper oriental tinting. Includes two oriental children, a fire screen, and paper fans. Minute white chip on lower right eye rim. Hands and legs have some repair and repainting. Otherwise body is in OK condition.
$1,500-$1,800

Shoulder Head
16" bisque shoulder head, marked "Simon Halbig," pierced ears, brown stationary eyes, open mouth with teeth, wearing a lace wedding dress.
$600-$700

Simon & Halbig
20" Simon & Halbig, marked "S 15 H 949," open mouth with teeth, blue eyes, fully jointed composition body, wearing a purple silk dress.
$2,250-$2,750

Porcelain Dolls

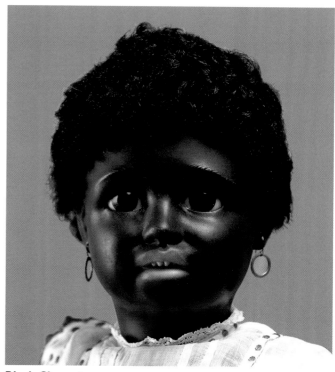

Brown Girl
20" German bisque brown S&H 1039 girl. Large brown stationary eyes, long human hair wig, and is on a fully jointed German body. Antique red dress with a later corduroy coat and hat. Fine scuffing to cheeks, teeth are chipped, and body is repainted.

$550-$650

Black Character
22" black S&H 1358 character. Brown set eyes on a jointed composition body. Wearing an antique white cotton dress with red polka dots, antique leather shoes, and an older curly black mohair wig (wig has not been removed from head). Minor wear at joints. Rare.

$10,000-$11,000

Lady
25" German bisque Simon and Halbig lady doll. Blue paperweight eyes, blonde mohair wig, and full-figured Simon and Halbig lady body. Frail maroon dress possibly original. Normal wear to joints. Shoes are newer replacements.

$1,200-$1,500

Bisque Head
26" bisque head, marked "CM Bergmann Simon Halbig 91/2," brown stationary eyes, open mouth with teeth, jointed composition body, pierced ears, blonde wig, wearing an aqua satin dress with white embroidered sheer coverlet.

$800-$1,000

Shoulder Head
26" bisque shoulder head, marked "S&H, DEP, Simon Halbig 1009," dark brown sleep eyes, open mouth with teeth, pierced ears, kid body, wearing a brown dress and hat.

$1,000+

Lady
26 1/2" German bisque S&H 1079 lady. On appropriate lady body, dressed in antique Gibson-style dress with human hair wig. Hairlines to side of face. Eyes have been glued in, but are now loose in head. Body retains its original finish with wear to hands.

$250-$350

Baby Blanche
28" bisque head (known as Baby Blanche), marked "Germany 1/2 S.& H. DEP 1079, Simon Halbig," pierced ears, large blue stationary eyes, open mouth with teeth, composition body, wearing a white cotton blouse and blue jumper.

$900-$1,100

Swivel Head
28" bisque swivel head on deep bisque shoulder plate, marked "S12H 1009 DEP, Simon Halbig" (slight scratch on cheek), blue threaded paperweight eyes, open mouth with teeth, blonde wig, kid body, bisque lade lower arms, wearing a green and black dress with black hat.

$1,500+

Simon & Halbig
31" Simon & Halbig, marked "CM Bergmann Simon & Halbig 14 1/2," blue sleep eyes, open mouth with teeth, pierced ears, blonde wig, fully jointed composition body, wearing a beige lace dress and straw bonnet.

$850-$1,000

Societe Francaise de Fabrication des Bébés et Jouets

The French Society for the Manufacture of Bébés and Toys is commonly referred to as S.F.B.J. In 1899, the society signed an agreement for locations in Paris and Montreuil-sous-Bois, France, establishing a syndicate to compete with German manufacturers.

Most of the best-known French firms joined the S.F.B.J., and continued to produce the same dolls that they had made as individual companies. Because so many different porcelain factories—using different molds—were involved, the quality of the products varies widely.

Two types of dolls were produced by S.F.B.J.: the familiar Bébés, and character dolls. The characters were modeled after real children with portrait-like detail as opposed to the idealized "dolly-face" Bébé. They were pouting, laughing, screaming, or smiling, as they portrayed baby or adolescent.

Googly

8" French bisque S.F.B.J. 245 Googly. Fully jointed composition body. Blue side-glancing stationary eyes. Newer blue and white mariner's costume. Red mohair wig and newer shoes. Slight ruddiness to bisque. Body in original paint.

$1,750-$2,000

Character Toddler

14" French bisque S.F.B.J. 247 character toddler. Blue sleep eyes, open/closed mouth with two molded teeth, on a jointed French toddler body. Dressed in a two-piece corduroy boy's suit with new human hair wig and replaced shoes. Hands are flaking with normal wear to rest of body. Light scuffing on cheeks and upper lip.

$900-$1,000

Character Box

S.F.B.J. French character box. Consisting of one complete doll (13 1/2") and two additional character heads with change of clothing in original display box. The mold number of the three dolls are: 237, 235, and 233. All have glass paperweight eyes and flocked hair. Lid of box has description in three languages of "The new interchangeable doll. Simple, clever and amusing." Box size: 19" by 14 1/2". Overall condition is virtually new. However, 235 & 237 characters have inherent factory mold lines at base of neck. Some minor paint flaking to composition ball-jointed body.

$3,800-$4,200/set

Character Baby

14" French bisque S.F.B.J. 242 character baby. Flocked hair, brown glass eyes, and an opening in mouth for drinking from original glass bottle. On a French composition baby body with original clothes. Flocking is sparse on the back of the head. Repaired eye chip on left eyelid with faint line going up towards forehead. Body has typical wear to fingers and joints.

$250-$350

French Bisque

15" French bisque S.F.B.J. 301. Dressed as a lady in black striped cotton. Original human hair wig and pate. On a jointed French composition body, wearing newer black and white leather shoes. Brown sleep eyes with some wax missing on the lids. Hands may have been replaced.

$300-$400

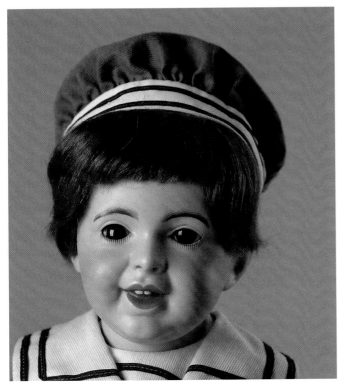

Character Baby

16" French bisque S.F.B.J. 236 character baby. Two molded teeth, brown sleep eyes, and brown mohair wig. Dressed in an older mariner's costume with newer shoes. On a five-piece S.F.B.J. baby body. Body has repair to fingers.

$280-$350

Character Baby

16" bisque head character baby ("Laughing Jumeau"), marked "S.F.B.J., 236, Paris 6", open mouth, painted teeth, brown sleep eyes, composition toddler body, wearing an off-white dress and bonnet.

$1,500-$1,600

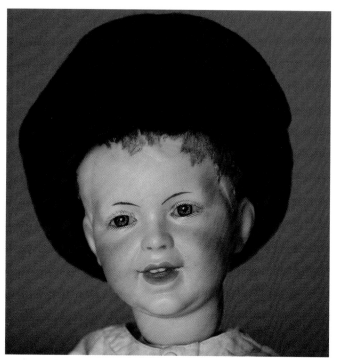

Character Boy
17" French S.F.B.J. 235 character boy with original box. Blue jeweled eyes with strawberry-blonde flocked hair (some loss to flocking), well molded facial features and fine bisque. Wearing original marked "AU BON MARCHE" shoes, on a jointed composition body. Original clothing (perhaps lacking coat) and an extra nightshirt. Overall condition is very fine original.
$1,200-$1,600

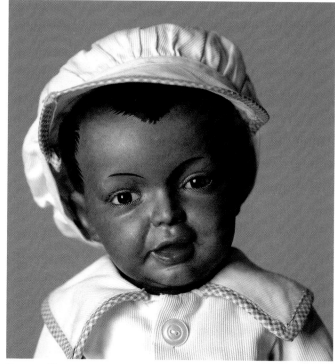

Brown Character Boy
17" French bisque S.F.B.J. 226 brown character boy. Painted hair and glass paperweight eyes and molded open/closed mouth. On a brown jointed French composition body and dressed in a three-piece boy's white and blue costume with antique oilcloth shoes. Body repainted.
$1,000-$1,300

Character Boy
17" French bisque S.F.B.J. 226 character boy. Painted hair and brown paperweight eyes with a molded open/closed mouth on a French composition body. Redressed in a brown terry cloth teddy bear romper. Light scuffing to cheek, some repair and repaint to body. Loosely strung.
$700-$800

Character Toddler
19" S.F.B.J. 252 character toddler. Wearing an antique gauze style dress with hat. Blue glass sleep eyes and a newer blonde curly mohair wig. Rear of head is marked "252." Wearing marked S.F.B.J. shoes marked "9." Body condition overall is very good with minor paint touch-up.
$4,000-$5,000

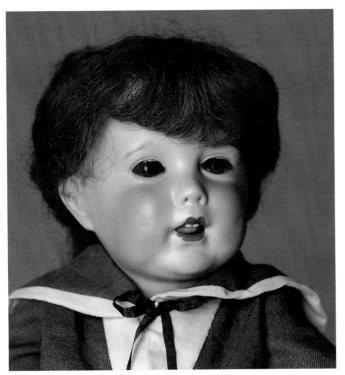

Character Toddler

19" French bisque S.F.B.J. 251 character toddler. With wobble tongue, and wearing a blue sailor suit. Blue sleep eyes with lashes, antique human hair wig, and fully jointed French toddler body. Body has repainting to lower arms and hands and typical wear at joints.

$350-$450

Character Boy

19" S.F.B.J. 227 character boy. Molded and painted hair with open mouth and teeth, blue jeweled eyes on a fully jointed French composition body (hands repainted). Wearing original sailor outfit (shoes replaced). Bisque is even and not high-colored, and marked "227" on back of head. Hairline to left side coming out of neck socket and extending 3" up to outside corner of eye. Old repair evident but not visible when doll is on display.

$350-$400

Character Boy

21" French bisque S.F.B.J. 233 character boy. On a jointed French body and dressed in a boy's two-piece red, white, and blue wool costume. Restoration to back of neck. Body retains original finish except repainting to hands.

$2,400-$2,700

Character Boy

21" French bisque S.F.B.J. 237 character boy. Redressed in brown velvet and ivory silk with replaced newer shoes. Blue paperweight eyes, on a jointed French body. Molded hair has overall repainting, and paperweight eyes need to be reset.

$1,000-$1,300

Character Boy

21" French bisque S.F.B.J. 235 character boy. Brown glass paperweight eyes, molded hair and open/closed mouth with two molded upper teeth. In crocheted sweater and hat with brown knickers. On a French fully jointed composition body with newer replacement shoes. Body has wear to lower legs and arms. Bisque has overall light speckling and a restoration to upper eyelid and brow.

$350-$450

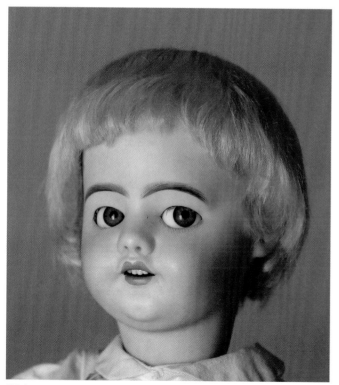

Girl

23" French bisque S.F.B.J. girl with flirty eyes. Blonde mohair wig, on a French jointed walker body with working crier. Hairline crack from neck socket in back, new clothes. Body has much wear to hands.

$125-$175

Jules Steiner, founded 1855

Based in Paris, many Steiner dolls are marked with the name "Bourgoin," a Paris merchant dealing in porcelains and associated with Jules Steiner during the 1880s. Sometime after 1897, Steiner purchased May Freres, Cie., the company responsible for the manufacture of Bébé Mascotte.

There is evidence that Steiner pressed its bisque doll heads even after other French manufacturers were routinely using the poured bisque method. Steiner Bébés have been found in sizes ranging from 8 1/2" to 38".

Dome Head Boy

14" bisque dome head boy, marked with an "S" inside an "H", intaglio painted blue eyes, closed mouth, old stick body, wearing a navy wool suit.

$300-$400

Bébé with Trunk
8" Steiner A Bébé with trunk. Original satin dress with blonde mohair wig and gauze hat. Trunk contains some original clothing and some newer clothing. On a five-piece composition body. Overall condition very fine.

$3,300-$3,800/set

Black Bébé
14" black open mouth Steiner A7 Bébé. On a fully jointed Steiner body with golden brown paperweight eyes, and original pate and knappy hair wig. Wearing an original lace and ribbon dress (dress has paper tag inside), and has a beaded necklace. Slight rub to tip of nose.

$2,000-$2,300

Steiner Bébé
17" Steiner series "C" Bébé. With dark brown paperweight eyes, mauve eye shadowing and expressive face. On a straight-wrist, jointed, composition Steiner body. Clothing and wig (sparse) are original and the shoes are antique. One wrist shows wear due to bracelet. Minute white scuff on left side of doll's cheek.

$3,500-$4,500

Steiner
20" Steiner A13, on a marked straight-wrist Steiner body. Dark brown human hair wig, wearing an off-white dress. Body has been over-glazed/painted but still retains original Steiner stamp on hip.

$2,000-$2,500

Steiner Bébé
21" Steiner A13 Bébé. Blue paperweight eyes, on a straight-wrist marked Steiner body with voice box. Wearing an ivory low-waisted blue and white eyelet dress, with antique leather shoes and a French human hair wig. Very fine condition.

$2,300-$2,700

Bébé Series C
23" Steiner Bébé Series C. Blue paperweight eyes, slight mauve shadowing. Wearing a white and blue eyelet dress, and an older replacement human hair wig and original cardboard pate. Body appears to be an old repaint.

$4,000-$5,000

Series G
24" Steiner Series "G." With bisque, wire eyes on marked straight-wrist Steiner body. Short blonde skin wig (replaced). Wearing antique cotton blue/gray dress with pinstripes, leather shoes, and velvet hat. Hairlines to bisque head and small eye chip on lower rim of left eye.

$4,000-$5,000

Steiner
25" Steiner Fire A15. With blue paperweight eyes and even complexion on a marked Steiner body. Wearing an antique silk dress, leather shoes, and a sandy human hair wig. Overall body is very good with some wear or minor touch-up. There are two pinprick black spots on tip of nose and a small black mark on forehead.

$3,000-$3,500

Steiner
28" A19 Steiner. Blue paperweight eyes, on a marked Steiner body. Wearing a frail antique child's dress with matching bonnet and a replacement human hair wig. Some wear to joints. Lower arms and hands have been repainted. Restoration to forehead does not involve facial features.

$3,000-$3,200

Swaine & Co., after 1910

Robert Swaine's porcelain factory in Hüttensteinach, near Sonneberg, Germany, produced dolls for only a short period of time. Swaine dolls have a green ink "GESTCHUTZT GERMANY S & Co." stamp, in addition to incised marks.

Character Girl
15" B.P. character girl by Swaine. Intaglio eyes, on a jointed composition body (hands repainted) and wearing regional clothing with a black floss wig. Rub marks on cheeks and nose, and some speckling to bisque.

$1,500-$1,800

A. Thuillier, active 1875 to 1893

Also known by the initialed mark "A.T.," François Gaultier provided at least some of the bisque heads used by Thuillier of Paris.

French Bébé

16" French Bébé "A. 5 T." with bulbous blue paperweight eyes and well-defined molding. On a Bru body with a Bru shoulder plate (Bru Jne #4). Wearing a blonde mohair wig with a cream satin dress highlighted with silk netting and antique boots. Repair to crack from neck socket going up through cheek to eye and continuing up to crown, restoration to right side of face. Rare.

$5,500-$6,500

Bébé

13" A. 3 T. Bébé. Brown paperweight eyes on a kid body with bisque lower arms. Marked on head and shoulder plate. Wearing an elaborate white cotton dress with lace trim and matching bonnet, highlighted by aqua ribbons on dress and hat. Antique leather shoes and sandy blonde mohair wig. Thumb repaired on right hand. Rare.

$19,000-$21,000

A. Thuillier Bébé

17" A. Thuillier Bébé. Bulbous blue threaded paperweight eyes, fine modeling. Marked "A. 6 T." on rear of head. Straight-wrist, eight ball-jointed body. Wearing antique shoes and chemise. Rare.

$25,000-$27,000

A. Thuillier Bébé

17" A. Thuillier Bébé. Marked on rear of head "A. 8 T.," on a proper style straight-wrist composition French body. Blue threaded paperweight eyes, antique shoes, underwear, and blonde mohair wig. Wearing a peach colored two-piece satin dress with some deterioration to fabric. Paint restoration to head, but does not involve any of the facial features.

$7,500-$8,500

A. Thuillier Bébé

22" A. Thuillier Bébé. Marked on rear of head "A. 9 T." On a straight-wrist appropriate French composition body. Dressed in an antique chemise, has an antique blonde mohair wig and blue paperweight eyes. Extensive restoration to the bisque head.

$3,000-$3,600

Thuillier Bébé

23 1/2" French A. 15 Thuillier Bébé. On a French jointed composition body. Pale bisque with mauve eye shadow is accentuated by her bulbous blue paperweight eyes (reset). Wearing a brown Bébé dress with matching hat, antique French shoes and socks, with leather gloves. Ash blonde mohair wig with shoulder-length curls. Body, although French, is not proper for this doll.

$24,000-$28,000

Van Rozen, active 1910 to 1914

A noted Belgian sculptor, J. Van Rozen designed doll heads in Paris. Her dolls are so rare that it is believed she created them as special commissions.

Van Rozen dolls are pressed, not poured, bisque, and are well marked with the Van Rozen name.

Black Character Boy
19" black smiling Van Rozen character boy. Dressed as a Marquis and has marked French shoes (with bumblebee) and is wearing a white powder human hair wig and a three-cornered hat. Fully marked on rear of head "VAN ROZEN, FRANCE DEPOSE." Open lips exposing molded teeth. Inset dark brown eyes that are highlighted with painted black eyelashes. Overall body condition fine, minor chipping at elbows and one finger has been repaired. Rare.

$12,000-$13,000

Adolf Wislizenus, after 1878

Adolf Wislizenus became sole owner in 1878 of a doll and toy factory that had been founded in 1851 in Waltershausen, Germany. After several ownership changes, the factory went out of business in 1931, and was acquired by König & Wernicke. Bähr & Pröschild, Simon & Halbig, and (after 1910) Ernst Heubach supplied bisque heads for A. Wislizenus dolls.

A.W. Special
23" German bisque A.W. Special. Brown sleep eyes, human hair wig, dressed in the Gibson Girl manner. On a fully jointed German body. Excellent condition.

$300-$400

Other Bisque-Head Dolls

From left: 5" all-bisque boy, all jointed brown glass eyes, brown hair, open mouth with teeth, painted stockings and shoes, wearing a brown suit. **$250+**

5 1/2" all-bisque, all jointed, marked "104 5 1/2" on head, brown glass eyes, closed mouth, painted shoes and socks, blonde wig, wearing a cream-colored dress. **$250+**

4 1/2" all-bisque, marked "German" on back, molded blonde hair, painted side-glancing eyes, all jointed, painted shoes and socks, wearing a lace dress. **$125+**

4 1/2" all-bisque, marked "3 Made in Germany," brown glass eyes, closed mouth, black wig, painted shoes and socks, wearing a violet lace dress. **$200+**

4 1/2" all-bisque, marked "5701 Made in Germany," blue glass eyes, closed mouth (slight repair on back), all jointed, red hair, painted shoes and socks. **$100+**

5" all-bisque, jointed, marked "Made in Germany," blonde wig, brown sleep eyes, open/closed mouth, painted shoes and socks, wearing a white lace dress. **$250+**

4" all-bisque, jointed, marked with a bell and "367 10" (possibly made by C. F. Kling & Co., 1836 to 1941), blue stationary eyes, brown wig, painted shoes and socks. **$200+**

4" all-bisque, marked "809 500 Germany," arms jointed at shoulders, painted blue eyes, closed mouth, blonde wig, painted shoes and socks, wearing a white dress with blue bonnet. **$150+**

4 1/2" all-bisque, marked "Made in Germany," brown painted eyes, closed mouth, painted shoes and socks, wearing a white dress. **$75+**

2 1/4" all-bisque jointed baby, marked "Germany," painted eyes and molded hair, wearing a white dress. **$50+**

3" all-bisque jointed baby, marked "Germany," painted eyes and molded hair, wearing a white dress. **$60**

Three 5" dolls, each with bisque heads and marked "German 70/12," blue glass eyes, mohair wigs, wood and composition bodies, molded shoes and socks, all in original clothing.

$250 each

Two 9 1/2" bisque Googlies, both marked "Demalcol 5/0 Germany" (a London firm, active 1921 to 1924, the name is an abbreviation of Dennis Malley & Co.), closed mouths, composition bodies, girl in pink dress and bonnet, boy in purple suit and hat.

$550-$650 each

11" French bisque Pierrot. Rear of head is marked with "LC" inside of anchor and "10/0" at base of neck. On a jointed five-piece composition body. White fired bisque and with multi-colored ornamentation, open mouth and brown eyes. Wearing an original red and cream silk outfit with cone-shaped hat. Silk outfit in frail condition, lacking shoes.

$200-$300

11" black bisque head, marked "SH 131 DEP," open mouth with teeth, brown stationary eyes, composition body, wearing an ecru dress, straw hat, brown stockings and leather shoes.

$700-$1,000

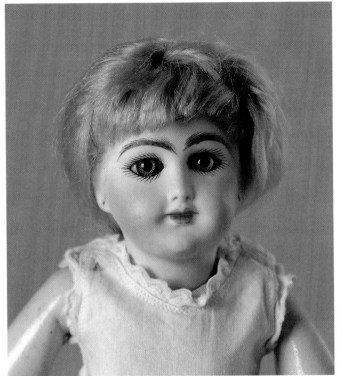

12 1/2" French "PAN" Bébé (probably by Henri Delcroix, late 1880s). Blue threaded paperweight eyes, pale bisque. On a straight-wrist, jointed composition French body. Original underwear, one shoe, and a French blonde mohair wig. Newer blue French-style dress. Minor wear to body.

$5,500-$6,500

13" bisque head, marked "Nippon, Japan," brown stationary eyes, open mouth with teeth, jointed baby body, wearing a pale blue cotton dress and cap.

$200-$250

14" bisque shoulder head, marked "8001 8/0," French look, possibly Kestner, brown stationary eyes, open mouth with teeth, blonde wig, body stuffed with excelsior, wearing an aqua and white tatted dress, black stockings, leather shoes.

$400-$500

14" bisque head, marked "OB," side-glancing glass eyes, open mouth with teeth, blonde wavy mohair wig, excellent composition body, wearing a pink taffeta coat and white dress.

$500+

14" bisque three-face doll, crying face with molded tears, brown stationary eyes, open mouths, old kid body, wearing a cream-colored lace baby dress and bonnet. **$2,000+**

15" French bisque shoulder head, marked "6," closed mouth, brown stationary eyes, kid body, wearing a black and green striped dress (shoulder plate has been repaired). **$800**

16" bisque shoulder head, marked "19" and a horseshoe and "Made in Germany," brown stationary eyes, open mouth with teeth, kid body, wearing a cotton dress with lace. **$200-$250**

16 1/2" Japanese bisque shoulder head, marked "5 ME Japan," blonde wig, brown sleep eyes, kid body, wearing aqua lace with aqua ribbons. **$250+**

17" bisque head, marked "M*B Japan 10," open mouth with teeth, blue stationary eyes, composition baby body, wearing an ecru net-embroidered dress. **$300-$400**

17" bisque turned shoulder head (repaired), unmarked, stationary blue eyes, closed mouth, kid body, wearing a black velvet embroidered dress. **As is, $500; if perfect, $1,000+**

18" bisque head, marked "Made in Germany Welsch" (probably Welsch & Co., 1911 to 1928), blue stationary eyes, open mouth with teeth, newer jointed body, wearing a maroon suit. **$300-$350**

19" French bisque character child. Brown sleep eyes, open mouth with two upper molded teeth, on jointed French body with blonde human hair braids, dressed in a blue and white dropped-waist cotton dress. Body has replaced legs repaired at joint. Some repair to fingers. Small eye chip to upper left lid, with hairline from corner of left eye. **$250-$350**

19" painted bisque swivel head, marked "Germany," blue sleep eyes, open mouth with teeth, composition body, dressed in blue bib overalls, white shirt, and leather shoes. **$300-$350**

20" bisque shoulder head, marked "Germany Mabel 4/0," closed mouth, blue stationary eyes, kid body (professionally repaired), bisque hands, blond curly wig, dressed in a white dress and pink and maroon bonnet.

$300-$350

21" Japanese bisque head character baby, marked "B 10 Nippon," brown stationary eyes, open mouth with teeth and tongue, fully jointed composition body, cream-colored romper (crack to nose).

$350+

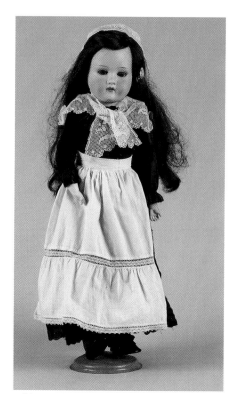

23" bisque shoulder head, marked "Germany Mabel 2" with "Flora Dora" marked on chest, blue sleep eyes, open mouth with teeth, kid body, wearing navy dress and apron.

$300-$350

24" French bisque character lady. Brown paperweight eyes, on a carved wood jointed lady body. Brown mohair wig, dressed in brown plaid silk and velvet-walking costume with high button replaced boots.

$1,500-$2,000

24" bisque head, marked "D Toft 1910," blonde wig, blue sleep eyes, distinctive jointed stick-type body, wearing a red dress with black trim.

$500+

24" bisque head, marked "M*13 Japan," blue stationary eyes, open mouth with teeth, jointed composition body, wearing a navy dress and a flowered hat with ribbon.

$350+

24" painted bisque swivel head, blue glass sleep eyes, open mouth with teeth, fully jointed composition body, dark brown wig, wearing a Gibson Girl-type dress with black belt and black leather shoes.

$200-$300

25" bisque swivel head on bisque deep shoulder plate, marked "939 S 13 H 941," blue paperweight eyes, open mouth with teeth, kid body, composition arms, wearing old lace over blue satin dress, white leather shoes.

$2,500+

26" French bisque-head, marked "33 Mon Tresor 12," (made by Henri Rostal, Paris, early 20th century), fully jointed toddler body, wearing a white dress and white leather shoes.

$4,000+

27" French bisque doll. Marked "V12G." Blue paperweight eyes with an open mouth and molded teeth, wearing a white antique dress (replaced ribbons) and antique white leather shoes. Cork pate and an antique human hair wig, on a fully jointed late French body. Light scuff to each cheek and minute chip on lower right eye rim. Body has fingernails painted on and retains original finish.

$450-$550

28" Japanese bisque head, marked "Nippon," brown stationary eyes, open mouth with teeth, long black hair, fully jointed body, wearing white eyelet dress and cap.

$500+

China-Head Dolls, 1840s to 1940s

Made for the most part in Germany, these glazed porcelain heads are difficult to attribute to specific manufacturers. They typically have molded and painted hair, painted eyes and eyelids, and a small, closed mouth.

Many china heads were sold without bodies. They fall into several categories, often identified by hairstyle: Bun, curly top, exposed ear, flat top, highbrow and lowbrow, spill curl, etc. Other terms include:

A "China Socket-style" head (where the head with neck fits into a shoulder plate or the opening of a body) is rare.

"English China" heads are flesh-colored or have a pink finish, with wigs, rather than painted hair.

"French China" heads often have glass eyes and wigs.

"Kinderkopf" refers to a china head representing a child.

Collector names (and descriptions) applied to china heads include:

Adelina Patti: elaborate hairstyle with center part and rolled curls; appropriately dressed. (1860s)

Alice (in Wonderland): hair styled with molded headband; appropriately dressed. (1850s)

Biedermeier: bald or solid dome head, some with top of head painted; good wig; appropriately dressed. (1840s)

Civil War (also known as flat-top or highbrow): hair styled with part in middle and short curls around head; appropriately dressed. (1850s)

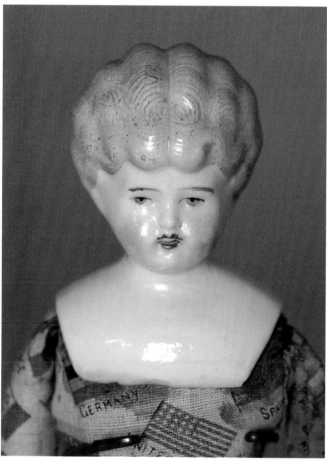

10" German china lady. 1890s-style china with blonde hair and seldom-seen open mouth. On a cotton flag print body with stone bisque lower arms and china lower legs. Body has some ink staining.

$120-$150

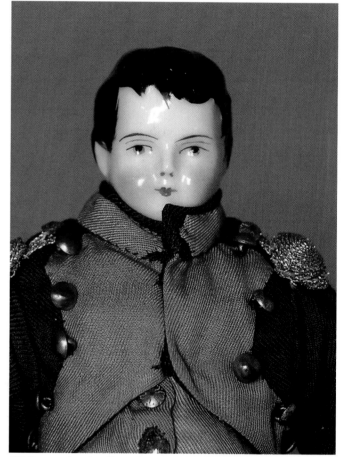

11" German china boy. Painted molded hair, blue painted eyes. On a kid body dressed in a handmade soldier's costume and wearing new leather shoes. Overall excellent condition.

$500-$600

From left: 11" china shoulder head (broken at neck), black molded hair, blue sleep eyes, bisque hands and legs, painted shoes, cloth body, wearing a pink dress.

$50+

13" china shoulder head "pet name," marked "Bertha" on shoulder plate in raised gold lettering, black molded hair, "kidolene" body, bisque hands, wearing a cream-colored dress.

$200+

12" china shoulder head "pet name," marked "Marian" on shoulder plate in raised gold lettering, cloth body stuffed with excelsior, china hands and lower legs, wearing a rose-colored dress.

$200+

13" French china lady. Blue painted eyes. On a French kid body, with braided mohair wig, and dressed in an older two-piece blue and gray iridescent silk costume, and antique underwear. Body appears to be in sturdy condition with some soiling.

$1,500-$1,800

14" china shoulder head (firing flaw on nose, head has been repaired), kid body, bisque hands, wearing a peach-colored dress.

$150+

15" German china, 1850s "covered-wagon" style doll. On cloth body with china limbs, fine painting, and pale blue eyes. Redressed in a handmade blue silk dress with lace trim. Small pepper mark on the tip of nose, upper portion of body and limbs appear to be antique, but cloth portion of legs are new.

$350-$400

15" German china Dressel and Kister man. Detailed wavy gray/brown hair and brows. On a newer cloth and leather body and costumed in newer fabrics. Replacement body seems sturdy.

$1,200-$1,600

15" French china Poupèe. Blue glass eyes, fine detailing to lashes and brows. Original sparse skin wig, on a leather French body. Wearing a hand-sewn two-piece cotton floral dress and newer straw hat. Small pepper mark near right brow.

$1,400-$1,800

15 1/2" German china Dressel and Kister lady. Painted gray hair and brows. On a cloth body with china limbs. Dressed in an ivory velvet two-piece gown. Shoulder plate needs to be sewn in place. Cloth body is of more recent vintage than head and limbs.

$1,100-$1,400

16" German KPM china lady with molded bun (Krister Porzellan Manufaktur AG, Bavaria, founded 1831). With dark brown painted hair pulled back in bun with exposed ears. Pale blue eyes. On an early cloth body wearing a two-piece hand-sewn red cotton dress and a newer black velvet cape. Some light speckling to face. Body is sturdy with some soiling and wear, especially to toes. Very light scuffing on back of bun.

$2,000-$2,500

16 1/2" KPM German china man (Krister Porzellan Manufaktur AG, Bavaria, founded 1831). Highly molded hair and fine facial detailing. On a cloth body with leather arms and wears shirt and pants. Shoulder plate is extensively restored but does not show above collar. Body is a newer replacement.

$1,500-$1,800

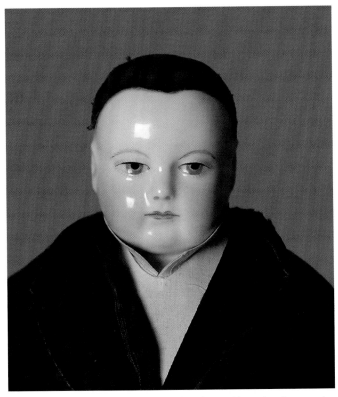

16 1/2" French china man. Molded eyelids, pale gray-blue painted eyes, and fine detail to lashes and brows. Kid body dressed in antique man's suit with "Boston" rubbers for shoes. Wig missing, overall excellent condition.

$5,800-$6,200

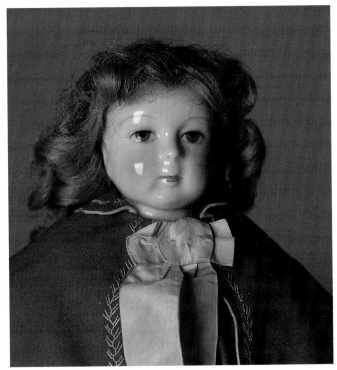

17" French china lady. Human hair wig and blue painted eyes. On a kid body with antique eyelet two-piece dress with red wool cape-style coat with featherstitch detailing, and antique white leather boots. Body has some repairs to arms and overall normal wear and soiling. Fine hairline approximately 1/2" going from crown towards right eyebrow.

$300-$400

Porcelain Dolls

17" French glass-eye china Poupèe, with eyeliner to top and bottom eyelids. In original frail costume with a letter of provenance stating that she was a Paris doll brought from Paris in 1860. On a sturdy body missing shoes and wig. Even glaze with one pit on left lower cheek.
$2,200-$2,800

17" china shoulder head (broken shoulder plate), blonde molded hair, blue eyes, cloth body, wearing a navy silk dress with lace collar.
As is, $50; if perfect, $250+

18" KPM German china lady (Krister Porzellan Manufaktur AG, Bavaria, founded 1831). With molded bun and exposed ears. On an old cloth body with red leather arms, wearing a red-checked homespun dress and original red leather slippers. Marked with a "7" on the back of her shoulder plate. Head has been reattached to body at some point. Firing crack at stringing hole on shoulder plate and another coming down to meet it, neither are visible when dressed. Minor scuffing to hair, cheek and forehead. Body is in good condition.
$2,000-$2,400

18" china shoulder head, rare brown eyes, black molded hair ("covered-wagon" style), slim, well-made cloth body, leather hands and leather buttoned shoes, wearing a cream-colored dress.
$800+

19" KPM German china lady (Krister Porzellan Manufaktur AG, Bavaria, founded 1831). Brown molded hair pulled back in bun. On a cloth body wearing a pink silk fashion dress with train. Small white spot on tip of nose and very light speckling on left cheek. Body is weak and needs repair. Fading to front of dress.

$5,800-$6,500

20" German china known as "Morning Glory." Braided molded bun with molded flower detailing behind each ear, and blue eyes. On an old cloth body with china limbs, dressed in antique cotton fabrics and antique underwear. Shoulder plate is extensively repaired and repair has yellowed. Costume has light soiling on sleeves and body has overall soiling with some repair.

$2,000-$2,500

21" German china lady, with brown eyes, 1860s molded black hairdo, on old cloth body with leather limbs. Dressed in an antique blue and brown cotton dress and antique underwear. Several small pepper marks to right side of face, minor scuffing on the hair in front and back. Leather limbs are in poor condition and left hand is missing. Stitched-on leather boots are missing the toes.

$150-$200

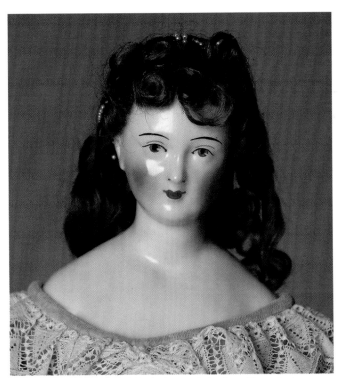

22" English pink-tint china lady. Antique mohair wig and long slender arms. Body is cloth with china limbs, wearing a newer peach velvet two-piece costume. Light speckling to face, deep pit center of forehead under the wig. Right thumb has been broken and reglued, right bisque leg is restored and repainted. New cloth body in sturdy condition.

$900-$1,200

Porcelain Dolls

23" china shoulder head, blue eyes, black molded hair, cloth body, china hands, wearing a silk dress.
$300+

24" German china lady, with brown eyes. 1860s, black hair with fine painting detail. On cloth body with china limbs. Original muslin dress and underwear. Lower right china leg has been broken and re-glued. Dress is soiled.
$400-$500

25" china shoulder head, blue eyes, black molded hair (firing flaw on chin), old cloth body, leather hands and sewed-on leather shoes, wearing a black silk dress with shawl.
$400+

28" china head, spill curl, blue eyes, cloth body, leather hands and shoes, dressed in olive green wool with black braid trim (back of shoulder plate broken).
As is, $175+; if perfect, $700+

31" china head, spill curl, original cloth body, leather hands, blue eyes, black hair, wearing a period brown cotton plaid dress with leather shoes that do not match.

$800+

33" china shoulder head boy, black molded hair, blue eyes, old cloth body, leather shoes and hands, wearing a black suit.

$500+

Parian-Head Dolls

First used in the mid-19th century, Parian is a creamy-white, slightly translucent porcelain, deliberately designed to look like the fine marble from the Greek island of Paros, which was used in classical times for important statues.

Various German porcelain factories produced Parian dolls from the late 1850s through the early 1880s, and Parian has become a generic term for the pale or untinted bisque dolls of the 19th century. Some may bear a number code, but most are unmarked.

Left, 4" Parian shoulder head, blonde molded hair, blue eyes, painted black ribbon in hair, all wooden jointed body, dressed in original red jumper, white blouse. **$300+**

Right, 6" milliner's model, all wood, painted face and black hair styled in a bun, all jointed body with painted legs and shoes, wearing a blue-gray cotton print dress.

$700+

Left, 9" Parian shoulder head, marked "131-9/2," molded blonde hair, painted eyes, cloth body, bisque hand and lower legs, brown painted shoes, wearing an aqua dress with white lace. **$200+**

Right, 12" Parian shoulder head, unmarked, molded blonde hair, blue painted eyes, old cloth body, leather hands, wearing an aqua satin and print dress.

$250+

16" German Parian with molded hair and feathers. Blue glass eyes, pierced ears and a molded decorated bodice with applied beading. On an old kid body with bisque hands, redressed in elaborate costume with a net and beading. Feather has some breaks and repair.

$350-$450

18" German Parian with molded hair. A "Dolly Madison" type with blue molded hair ribbon, painted and decorated shoulder plate, and blue painted eyes. On a cloth body with older replacement cotton dress. Hands missing, lower legs in fragile, poor condition.

$600-$700

21" German Parian man with molded shoulder plate. Shoulder plate has molded blue polka-dot tie with gold highlighting. On cloth body with leather arms, wearing a man's suit and antique oilcloth shoes. Costume is frail, body and hands are sturdy.

$450-$550

21" Parian shoulder head, blue stationary eyes, blonde molded hair, kid body, bisque hands, closed mouth, wearing an old yellow wool dress.

$200+

23" Parian shoulder head, blonde molded hair, cloth body, bisque hands and feet, wearing a gold velvet dress.

$100+

Synthetic Materials

Celluloid, Hard Plastic, Latex, Rubber, Vinyl

Though this category covers a wide range of materials used for doll manufacture—starting in the second half of the 19th century and continuing today—all of these man-made products have one thing in common: Each was an attempt to make dolls faster, cheaper, more realistic, and longer lasting. As you will see, the results—especially regarding durability—are mixed.

Celluloid

Celluloid is a brittle, flammable thermoplastic composed mainly of cellulose nitrate and camphor.

Originally a trademark, celluloid was produced in Europe, the United States, Japan, and other countries from the late 1860s until about 1950. Many companies produced celluloid dolls or celluloid doll parts, including Le Minor, Parsons Jackson, Kämmer & Reinhardt, Petitcollin, Kestner, Averill, Irwin, Marks, and Rheinische Gummi, which claimed it was the first to manufacture celluloid dolls.

Marks include an embossed stork (Parsons-Jackson), turtle (Schultz), Indian head (American), mermaid (Cellba), beetle or ladybug (Hernsdorfer-Germany), star (Hollywood), SNF (Société Nobel Francaise), ASK (Zast of Poland). For additional marks, refer to Antique Trader's Doll Makers and Marks by Dawn Herlocher.

In 1908, Playthings Magazine reported, "...prior to 1905, celluloid dolls were clumsy looking and could not withstand the knocking about that children gave them. Between 1905 and 1908, celluloid dolls improved in appearance and durability. Most of the Celluloid Dolls were made in Germany but many of them were painted by girls in Italy. All types of boys and girls were represented in celluloid dolls."

Production of celluloid was halted in the United States during the 1940s because of its tendency to burn or explode if placed near an open flame or high heat.

Because they are easily broken and become quite brittle, proper care helps a perfect celluloid example remain that way. Keep these dolls in a cool room with good ventilation and, because it is highly combustible, never store celluloid in a sealed case.

Celluloid dolls are often grouped into several categories, rather than by manufacturer. Condition, including discoloration, has a significant effect on value.

All Celluloid: jointed at neck, shoulder, and hip, or bent-limb baby body; molded hair or good wig; painted eyes; dressed or undressed; marked or unmarked.

All Celluloid: molded in one-piece or jointed at shoulders only; molded and painted hair and facial features; dressed, undressed, or molded clothing; often pink in color; marked or unmarked.

Better Quality, Socket Head: dolly, character, or baby face; composition-and-wood body; mohair or human hair wig; glass eyes; applied lashes and brows; closed or open mouth with teeth; appropriately dressed; typically marked by various manufacturers, such as Käthe Kruse, Kämmer & Reinhardt, and others.

Celluloid, Shoulder Head: cloth or kid body; celluloid or composition arms; molded and painted hair or good wig; glass or painted eyes; closed mouth or open mouth with teeth (often made of cardboard); appropriately dressed; marked or unmarked.

2 3/4" celluloid wedding couple, marked "Japan," painted eyes, in original outfits.
$70-$100/pair

3" celluloid twins with pacifier, marked on back with a turtle, original pink and blue outfits.
$70 to $100/pair

From left: 5 1/2" celluloid Jackie Coogan painted rattle doll.
$40-$50

Celluloid mechanical crawling baby, with painted blue eyes, all original.
$50+

6" celluloid baby, marked with a turtle and "16/1/2," painted eyes, nurser mouth with tiny pacifier around neck.
$15+

From left: 7 1/2" celluloid carnival Kewpie, marked on back "GK" in a circle, painted features, side-glancing eyes, painted shoes, with original feathers and cane.
$25-$50

8 1/2" German celluloid children, Hansel and Gretchen (#5934 and 5964), marked with a turtle in a diamond, jointed, marked "Made in Germany," in German outfits of felt, cotton, and leather, all original.
$100-$200 each

8" celluloid rattle girl, dressed in red and white.
$25-$40

9" celluloid doll, blue painted eyes, painted socks and shoes, wearing original traditional peasant outfit, tagged "Moll-6 origin TRACHTEN-Puppen."

$60-$90

10" celluloid doll with jointed body, all original, tagged "Samaritaine Deluxe Paris."

$60-$90

13" celluloid head football player with Harvard "H," molded helmet, painted eyes, body stuffed with excelsior.

$50-$100

Left, 17" all celluloid jointed doll, marked with a turtle and "Schultz-Marae #43," molded hair, blue painted eyes, painted shoes and socks, wearing a white eyelet baby dress.

$150+

Right, 12" all celluloid baby, marked with a stork (Parsons-Jackson, American, active 1910 to 1919), jointed body, blue painted eyes, open mouth with painted teeth, wearing a cream-colored embroidered net dress.

$200+

19" celluloid head boy, marked "K(star)R 728-7 Germany 43/46," glass stationary eyes, open mouth with teeth, composition body, wearing a black velvet jacket, white straw hat and leather shoes.

$300-$350

Hard Plastic, Latex, Rubber, Vinyl

27" painted celluloid swivel head, blue glass sleep eyes, open mouth with teeth and tongue, marked with a turtle and "47" on the neck, all composition jointed body, blonde wig with braids, wearing a white cotton dress and blue bonnet.

$350-$450

When it was discovered that the milky white fluid produced by various seed plants—also known as latex—could be processed, it became the source of rubber, and was later synthesized.

In 1837, Charles Goodyear received his first patent for a process that made rubber easier to work with. In 1843, Goodyear discovered that if sulfur was removed from rubber, then heated, it would retain its elasticity. This process called vulcanization made rubber waterproof and opened the door for an enormous market of rubber goods.

In the first half of the 20th century, plastics came into their own.

In 1909, inventor Leo Baekeland unveiled the world's first fully synthetic plastic—Bakelite—at a meeting of the New York chapter of the American Chemical Society. It could be fashioned into molded insulation, valve parts, pipe stems, billiard balls, knobs, buttons, knife handles, and all manner of items.

During the early 1920s, a scientist named Waldo Semon stumbled onto a new material during his search for a synthetic adhesive. He experimented by making golf balls and shoe heels out of the material called polyvinyl chloride, or PVC.

But it wasn't until the late 1940s that plastics, rubber, and vinyl emerged as the basis for modern mass-produced dolls.

Hard Plastic, Latex, Rubber, Vinyl doll makers

Alexander Doll Co., founded 1923

A true American success story, the company was established by the Alexander sisters—Beatrice Alexander Behman, Rose Alexander Schrecking, Florence Alexander Rapport, and Jean Alexander Disick. Their parents, Russian immigrants Maurice and Hannah Alexander, owned and operated the first doll hospital in the United States.

In 1929, a line of dolls appeared in trade catalogs advertised as "Madame Alexander." The following year the Alexander sisters expanded this line, now commonly known as "Madame Alexander Dolls." (Also see cloth, composition.)

Madame Alexander Dolls come in more than 6,500 different costumed personalities, so it's important to have the original costume and/or wrist tag to properly identify the dolls.

Little Genius
Two 7 1/2" Madame Alexander "Little Genius" dolls, hard plastic jointed bodies, blonde karakul wigs, bottle mouth, redressed.

$125+ each

Groom
17" Madame Alexander hard-plastic groom. In original clothing. Small scuff on left cheek.

$200-$250

Madame Alexander
17" Madame Alexander doll, hard plastic, sleep eyes, unmarked, wearing a red and white dress.

$250-$275

Little Women
14" Little Women doll, hard plastic, sleep eyes, closed mouth, jointed body, original red and white striped cotton dress.

$130+

Bride and Groom
7 1/2" Madame Alexander bride and groom, hard plastic jointed bodies, all original, dress marked "Wendy Kin, Madame Alexander."

$200+ each

Godey Lady
20" Madame Alexander Godey Lady, blue sleep eyes, head marked "Madame Alexander 1961," dress marked "Godey, Madame Alexander, NY, USA."

$250+

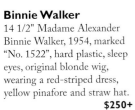

Binnie Walker
14 1/2" Madame Alexander Binnie Walker, 1954, marked "No. 1522", hard plastic, sleep eyes, original blonde wig, wearing a red-striped dress, yellow pinafore and straw hat.

$250+

Cissy
20" Madame Alexander Cissy, hard plastic, all jointed including knees, sleep eyes, original hairdo, blue formal and fur.

$600+

American Character Doll Co., 1919 to 1968

Located in New York, the firm started with composition dolls and later made a range of hard plastic and vinyl dolls. (Also see composition.)

Betsy McCall
8" Betsy McCall, jointed vinyl, sleep eyes, rooted hair, wearing original skating attire.

$125+

Betsy McCall
13" Betsy McCall, head marked 1956, vinyl jointed body, wearing original blue cotton dress.

$100+

Betsy McCall
14 1/2" vinyl-head doll marked "Betsy McCall Corp., Ideal P-90," hard plastic jointed body, brown sleep eyes, redressed.

$150+

Sweet Sue
14" American Character
Sweet Sue, all hard plastic,
jointed body, strawberry
blonde hair, redressed in
cotton checked dress.
$100-$125

Sweet Sue
15" American
Character Sweet
Sue, hard plastic
jointed body,
blonde wig,
redressed.
$100+

Sweet Sue
20" American Character Sweet
Sue, hard plastic, sleep eyes,
jointed body, strawberry blonde
hair, redressed in cotton print
rickrack dress.
$150-$175

Sweet Sue
23" American Character Sweet
Sue, hard plastic, sleep eyes,
jointed body, sailor suit, black
and white shoes (possibly all
original).
$200-$225

Tiny Tears

13" American Character Tiny Tears, hard plastic head marked with patent number 20675644, bottle mouth and tear ducts, vinyl jointed body, all original.

$100-$125

American Character

14" American Character doll, all hard plastic, gray sleep eyes, original styled hair and outfit.

$100-$125

15" American Character doll, all hard plastic, green sleep eyes, red rooted hair in cap on head, closed mouth, redressed.

$100-$125

15" marked American Character doll, all hard plastic, blue sleep eyes, rewigged, jointed body, dress (possibly original) with white organdy over blue slip.

$100-$125

17 1/2" American Character doll, hard plastic, jointed body blue-gray sleep eyes, dress may be original.

$150+

18" American Character doll, all hard plastic, jointed body, sleep eyes, closed mouth, original taffeta plaid dress and hat.

$150-$175

Whimsie
20" Whimsie character, marked "American Doll and Toy Corp., 1960 Series," dressed in black cap and gown with diploma.

$80-$100

24" American Character bride, all hard plastic, jointed body, blue sleep eyes, original wedding dress and veil; mint.

$200-$225

24" American Character doll, vinyl head, hard plastic body with pin-jointed knees, sleep eyes, closed mouth, original cotton print dress.

$200-$225

24" American Character doll, unmarked, hard plastic, open mouth with teeth, green sleep eyes, wearing white blouse and red skirt.

$200-$225

24 1/2" American Character doll, all hard plastic, jointed body, sleep eyes, closed mouth, strawberry blonde hair, wearing original pink rayon and net dress, white shoes, with flowers in hair and at waist.

$200-$225

Jointed Body
17 1/2" R&B hard plastic jointed body, sleep eyes, original gold shoes, green net dress, with green flowers on dress and in hair.

$150+

Eegee, founded 1917

Mr. and Mrs. E. Goldberger founded this company in Brooklyn, N.Y. The trademark EEGEE was adopted in 1923. Early dolls were marked "EG," followed by "E. Goldberger," and finally "Eegee" or occasionally "Goldberger." (Also see composition.)

Groucho Marx
32" Groucho Marx ventriloquist doll, marked "Eegee Co.," vinyl head and hands, cloth body.
$100+

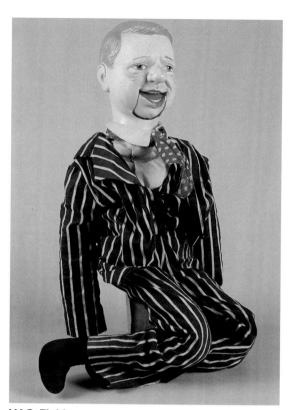

W.C. Fields
32" W.C. Fields ventriloquist doll, marked "Eegee Co." (circa 1980), vinyl head and hands, cloth body, missing hat (?).
$70+

Effanbee Doll Co., founded circa 1910

Effanbee is an acronym for Fleischaker & Baum, New York. The firm's Patsy doll was the first realistically proportioned American-made doll designed to resemble a real child. She was also the first doll for which companion dolls were created, and the first to have a wardrobe and fan club. In 1934, Effanbee introduced "Dydee," the first drink-and-wet doll. The company also imported and distributed cloth display or souvenir dolls made in Spain by Klumpe. (Also see composition.)

Honey
16" Honey doll, hard plastic jointed body, sleep eyes, original brown hair and clothing, including pink leather shoes and white socks; mint condition.
$350+

Hasbro®, Inc., founded 1923

The company was originally known as Hassenfeld Bros., founded by Henry and Hillel Hassenfeld in Pawtucket, R.I. The family-owned-and-operated toy business adopted the familiar Hasbro name following a division in the company. One branch went into the pencil box business, the other into the toy business.

In 1962, Hasbro's creative director, Don Levin, was approached by a television producer to develop a line of toys based on a pending television program about soldiers. The first G.I. Joe was introduced in 1964, and had 21 movable parts and realistic hair. He was named after the title character in the movie The Story of G.I. Joe. From the start, realism, simplicity, price, and a seemingly endless supply of accessories contributed to the success of the G.I. Joe figures. There are reportedly more than 500 G.I. Joe figures, vehicles, and auxiliary items.

Production of G.I. Joe figures was suspended in 1978 due to an increase in the price of petroleum, a major component in the manufacturing of G.I. Joe. Hasbro currently offers new G.I. Joes in 3 3/4" and 12" sizes, along with dozens of related accessories. (For more information, go to Hasbro.com.)

12" Hasbro G.I. Joes, including black adventurer with flocked hair, 1970, #7404, in tan Army fatigues; bandaged soldier with stretcher and medical equipment; and painted-hair Joe, 1964, in camouflage uniform. All three have scars on cheeks (only Action Soldiers of the nation do not have a scar). Shown with footlocker made by Hassenfeld Bros., 1965.

Figures, $125-$300 each

Flocked-hair bearded Adventure Soldier in Army camouflage,
$100+

Atomic Man Mike Powers, with clear-plastic arm and leg, and flashing eyes,
$125+

Radio Commander talking Action Soldier, painted hair,
$100+

Painted-hair Search and Rescue soldier,
$100+

Left:

Flocked-beard Adventure Soldier in fighter pilot outfit,

$100+

Action Nurse (sold in Montgomery Ward 1967 catalog for $4.99), blonde rooted hair,

$1,000+

Painted-hair soldier in demolition or emergency rescue outfit,

$100+

Painted-hair marine Action Soldier,

$100+

Bearded flocked-hair sailor in Shore Patrol outfit,

$100+

Blond painted-hair rescue diver Action Soldier,

$120+

Flocked-hair bearded Adventure Soldier in military police outfit,

$100+

Russian infantry soldier (no scar) painted hair (Action Soldier of the World),

$200+

Talking Action Sailor, painted hair,

$125+

Secret agent outfit, including mask disguise, on painted-hair Action Soldier,

$160+

Action Soldier in Jungle Fighter Outfit,
$125+
Painted-hair Action Soldier in regimental army fatigues,
$125+
Flocked-beard Adventure Soldier in Landing Signal Officers outfit,
$100+
Flocked-beard Adventure Soldier in regimental army fatigues,
$100+

E.I. Horsman & Co., founded 1865

This well-known maker was founded in New York by Edward Imeson Horsman. Beginning in the early 1900s, Horsman produced a variety of popular composition dolls.

Horsman is famous for marketing the Billiken doll, originally created by Florence Pretz of Kansas City, Mo. It is reported that during the first six months of production, Horsman sold more than 200,000 Billikens. (Also see composition.)

Horsman Girl
15" hard plastic girl, circa 1952, marked "Horsman" on head, blue sleep eyes, open mouth with teeth, original wig, wearing a cotton print dress.
$100-$150

LuAnn Simms
20 1/2" Horsman doll marked "LuAnn Simms," hard plastic, sleep eyes, open mouth with teeth, black hair, original red dress and white shoes.
$100-$125

Ideal® Novelty and Toy Co., founded 1902

Morris Mitchom and A. Cohn founded the company initially to produce Mitchom's teddy bears.

Ideal was one of the few large companies that made its own composition dolls. The company pioneered the so-called "unbreakable" dolls in America. American Character, Arranbee, Eugenia, and Mary Hoyer were among Ideal's customers. (Also see composition.)

Ideal began experimenting with hard plastic in 1936 and was the first to market a hard-plastic doll, resulting in Toni and the Play Pal Family. Play Pal children were designed according to measurements issued by the U.S. Bureau of Standards of Specifications. They could wear the clothing of a child at the age of three months, one year, two years, three years, and an older child of 10 or 11 years.

The first plastic doll was manufactured by Ideal in 1940, but was discontinued due to war restrictions on materials. Ideal's patent number for hard plastic was #2252077, and many different dolls can be found marked with this number.

Ideal Dolls
14" Ideal doll, marked "P-90 Made in USA," all hard plastic, rewigged, sleep eyes, wearing an aqua satin and lace dress.

$125-$150

14" Ideal doll, marked "P-90 Made in USA" on head and back, blonde hair, blue sleep eyes, all hard plastic jointed body, wearing a majorette outfit in white, red and gold.

$125-$150

Toni
14 1/2" Ideal Toni, marked "P-91," blue sleep eyes, hard plastic, jointed body, dress may be original.

$125-$150

14 1/2" Ideal Toni, marked "P-90," sleep eyes, blonde hair, hard plastic, jointed body, wearing original white blouse and black skirt.

$125-$150

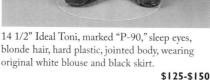

15" Ideal doll, marked "391 USA" (Toni doll), all hard plastic, jointed body, wearing copy of original red and white dress, red shoes.

$125-$150

15" Ideal doll P-91 (Toni doll, Sarah?), dress may be original.

$125-$150

Toni
15" Ideal Toni doll, marked "P-91 Made in USA," all hard plastic, jointed body, sleep eyes, blonde hair, may be original red checked dress.

$125-$150

16" Ideal doll, marked "P-91," hard plastic, blue sleep eyes, closed mouth, wearing a blue dress.

$125-$150

Harriet Hubbard Ayers
16" Harriet Hubbard Ayers doll, head marked "Ideal, 16-P91," wearing original wedding dress and veil.

$125+

Revlon
17 1/2" Ideal VT-18 Revlon doll, vinyl jointed body marked "Ideal," high heels and original peach-colored dress.

$100+

Bride
21" Ideal bride, P-93 (Toni family), hard plastic, blue sleep eyes, jointed body, wearing original wedding dress and veil.

$250-$275.

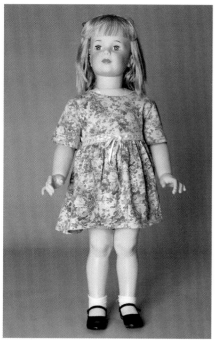

Patty Play Pal
36" Patty Play Pal in original box. Near mint vinyl doll in print dress with underwear, socks and shoes, blonde hair with red ribbon. Extremely bright facial coloring. Dress has slight soiling. Box is in good condition with tape marks and slight distressing.

$850-$950

Shirley Temple
15" vinyl Shirley Temple, marked "Ideal ST-15" on head, sleep eyes, rooted hair.

$225+

Shirley Temple
15" vinyl Shirley Temple, marked "Ideal ST-15" on head, brown sleep eyes, open mouth with teeth, possibly original outfit.

$225+

Shirley Temple
16" vinyl Shirley Temple, marked "1972 Ideal Toy ST-14 Corp., Hong Kong" and "1972-5638," stationary eyes, painted mouth, rooted hair, wearing original white dress with red dots.

$275-$325

Kenner Parker Toys, Inc.

In 1985, Kenner became an independent company with two divisions, Parker Brothers and Kenner products. Kenner was once a subsidiary of General Mills. They produced many dolls as well as popular action figures.

Blythe
11 1/2" Blythe character doll, hard plastic head, vinyl body, marked "Blythe TM Kenner Prod., 1972, General Mills," pull string operates mechanism that changes color of eyes from brown to green to blue, in original red dress (poor condition).

$60

Mattel® Inc.,

In 1945, Mattel established its headquarters in Hawthorne, Calif. The company, founded by Harold Matson and Elliot Handler, derived its name from a combination of letters from the two partners' names.

Mattel, the world's largest toy manufacturer, is probably best known for Barbie, along with her friends and family. Initially Mattel produced dollhouse furniture. They expanded to include music boxes, toy guns, and a host of dolls such as Chatty Cathy, Sister Bell, Baby First Step, Cheerful-Tearful, Dancerina, and Talking Mrs. Beasley.

Chatty Cathy Sister
17" hard plastic Chatty Cathy Sister, marked "Mattel, Singing Chatty, 1964," dressed in original aqua and white dress and shoes.
$50+

Tiny Chatty Baby
14" Tiny Chatty Baby, vinyl, sleep eyes, original blue outfit.
$40+

Chatty Cathy
20" Chatty Cathy, marked "Mattel," blue sleep eyes, dark rooted hair, wearing original red jacket, white dress and shoes.
$100+

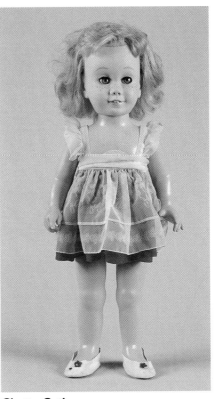

Chatty Cathy
20" Chatty Cathy, jointed vinyl, blonde hair, blue sleep eyes, talker with pull string (not working).
$85+

Charmin' Chatty
24" Mattel talking "Charmin' Chatty" with original box. Blonde doll wearing red, white and blue sailor's outfit. When pulling cord on back, "Charmin' Chatty" talks (recording slightly unclear). Outfit has some soiling.
$100-$125

Ken & Barbie
Boxed Ken & Barbie, and another Barbie with detached head and many articles of clothing and accessories including three wigs. Fair to good condition.
$350-$450/set

Barbie, Ken & Midge
Barbie, Ken & Midge parade set with original box. In fine original condition (Barbie has green oxidation at earring holes). Box shows wear to lid and there is taping to corners.
$850-$950/set

The Pleasant Co., founded 1985

The Pleasant Co. was founded in 1985 by author-educator Pleasant T. Rowland in Middleton, Wis. Rowland created the American Girl line of dolls, which also includes books and accessories. Mattell acquired the company in 1998.

Molly
Pleasant Co. American Girl "Molly" with accessories. Variety of clothes, bed, dining room table and two chairs, birthday party settings, books, etc. Doll 18" tall. Like new, in boxes.

$750-$850/set

Kristen
Pleasant Co. American Girl "Kristen" with accessories. Variety of clothes, blue wooden trunk, dining room table, place settings, books, and accessories. Doll 18" tall. Like new, in boxes.

$850-$950

Samatha
Pleasant Co. American Girl "Samatha" with accessories. Variety of clothes, wicker table, stroller, service setting, brass bed, cloth covered dome trunk, books, and accessories. Doll 18" tall. Like new, in boxes.

$800-$900

Sasha Dolls, founded 1964

Designed by Swiss artist Sasha Morgenthaler (1893-1975), her dolls were mass-produced by Götz-Puppenfabrik, Rödental, Germany, beginning in 1964. Morgenthaler transferred the licensing rights to Trenton (sometimes spelled Trendon) Toy Ltd., Reddish, Stockport, England, which continued producing Sasha Dolls until the company went out of business in 1986.

The Gotz Dolls were marked "Sasha Series" within a circle on the back of the head. Also, the upper eyelids of the Gotz dolls are painted with a curved eyelid. Other Sasha Dolls are painted with a straighter eyelid line. All Sasha Dolls have a realistic body construction, allowing for a range of movement. Later Sasha dolls are unmarked except for a wrist tag.

A limited-edition series of dolls was produced between 1981 and 1986.

In 1995, Gotz again started making Sasha Dolls. The new Sashas, although similar in appearance to the earlier dolls, are marked with an incised circular logo between the shoulders, and the neck is incised "Gotz."

Sasha Black Baby
11" Sasha black baby. Black nappy hair with a white outfit, wrist tag, and original box. All original condition.

$100-$125

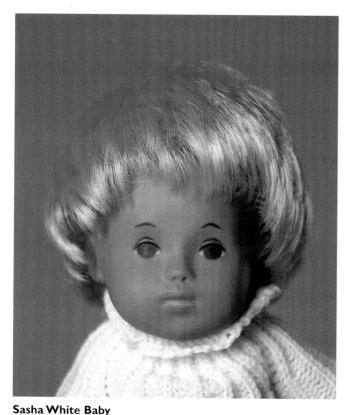

Sasha White Baby
11" Sasha white baby. Blonde hair with knit white outfit, wrist tag, and original box. All original condition.

$85-$125

Trenton Sasha
16" Trenton Sasha with red hair. All original, with box in excellent condition.

$185-$225

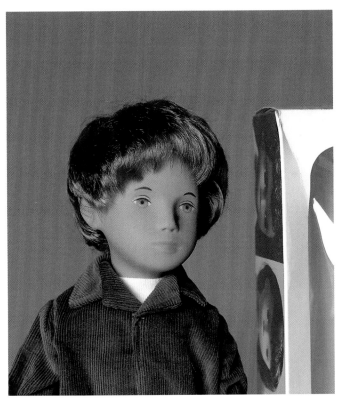

Trenton Sasha Gregor
16" Trenton Sasha Gregor with red hair. All original, with box in excellent condition.

$150-$200

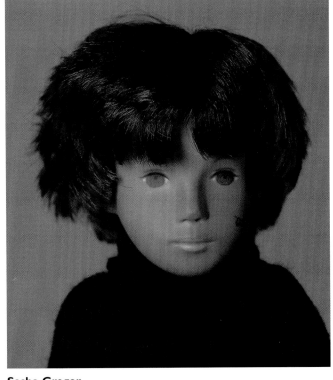

Sasha Gregor
16" Sasha "Gregor." Dark brown hair, knit sweater, denim trousers, wrist tag in original cylinder container. Print mark on cheek, probably from catalog that was stored in box.

$100-$125

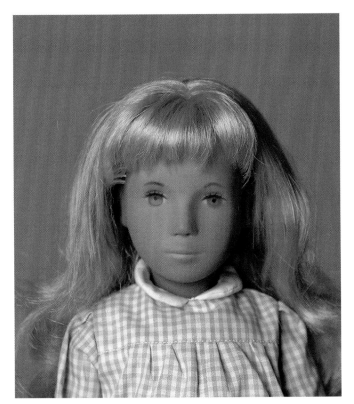

Sasha Girl
16" Sasha girl. Long blonde hair, blue and white gingham romper, original wrist tag in original cylinder container. Overall fine condition.

$300-$400

Black Cora
16" Trenton Sasha black Cora. All original, in original box with some yellow spots on dress.

$100-$125

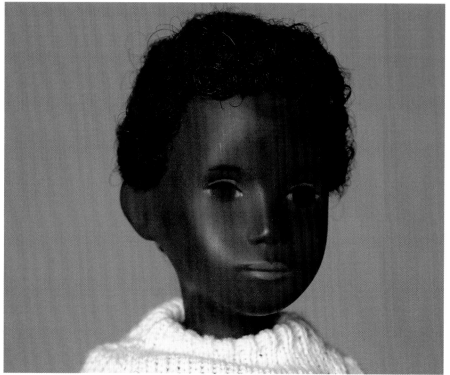

Black Caleb
16" Trenton Sasha black Caleb. All original. Yellow spots on pants.

$100-$125

Mary Jane
16" Mary Jane doll, made by G.H. & E. Freydberg Inc. in 1953, hard plastic, green eyes.

$175+

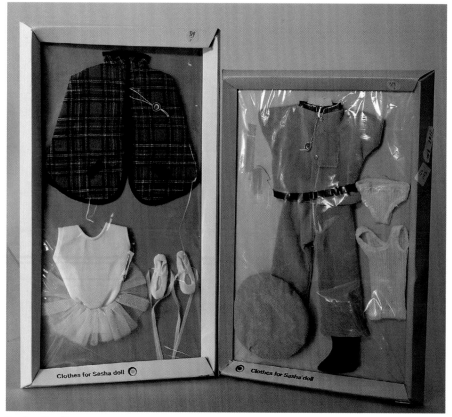

Sasha Outfits
Seven Sasha outfits. Six with wrist tags, and boxes; seventh outfit has no box and is a leather romper with matching boots and wrist tag. Overall fine.

$400-$500/set

Baby Linda Lee
8 1/2" Baby Linda Lee, hard plastic, jointed baby body, painted eyes, wearing original blue top, with coat and hat.

$150-$175

Terri Lee Co., 1946 to 1958

Violet Gradwohl established the company in Lincoln, Neb. The first dolls were made of composition, and later hard plastic.

Gradwohl received a patent for a process used to create artificial hair wigs woven from Celanese yarn. She also designed the clothing with her daughter, Terri Lee, for whom the dolls were named.

A brother, Jerri Lee; sister, Baby Linda; and friends Bonnie Lu, Patty Jo, Benjie, and Nanooh (an Eskimo child) were introduced. All the dolls used the same basic doll mold—the only difference was wig types or facial painting. There are also a 10" Tiny Terri Lee and Tiny Jerri Lee, and a doll called Connie Lynn.

When the Terri Lee Doll Co. factory in Lincoln was destroyed by fire, the firm relocated to Apple Valley, Calif.

Several copies of Terri Lee dolls have been produced. Many were made during the early 1950s at the peak of Terri Lee's popularity. They often have holes in their feet.

Tiny Terri Lee
10" Tiny Terri Lee, hard plastic, brown painted eyes, strawberry blonde hair, wearing original plaid dress.
$125+

Tiny Jerri Lee
10" Tiny Jerri Lee, hard plastic, painted eyes, wearing original cowboy outfit, red vest, black shorts, boots.
$125+

Terri Lee Bride
16" Terri Lee bride (1951), blonde hair, original dress and veil.
$275+

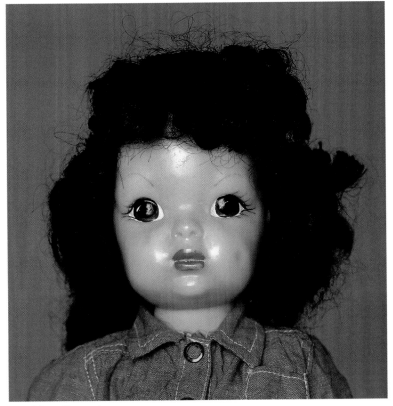

Terri Lee Brownie
16" Terri Lee Brownie, 1950s. Buckle and part of leather missing from belt. Wear to lips.
$125-$175

Jerri Lee
16" Jerri Lee, hard plastic, jointed body, brown painted eyes, fur hair, wearing original fireman's hat and saddle shoes.

$200-$250

Jerri Lee
16" Jerri Lee with karakul hair, painted eyes, wearing original cowboy outfit and boots.

$200+

Vogue Dolls, Inc., founded circa 1918

Jennie H. Graves started the company in Somerville, Mass., focusing on the production of doll clothing until the mid-1930s. Graves then bought undressed bisque dolls from German manufacturers, dressing them in her designs, and reselling them.

In 1948, the Ginny-type doll was introduced as a composition doll, known as "Toddles." (Also see composition.)

Several Vogue Dolls were originally Arranbee Dolls. Vogue purchased Arranbee in 1957, but the dolls continued to be marked and sold as Arranbee until as late as 1961.

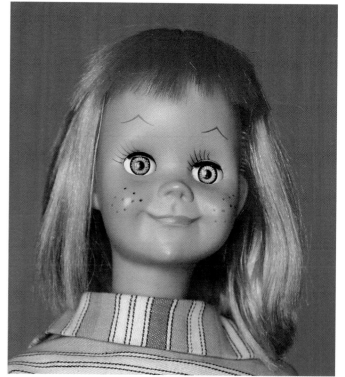

Brickette
22" vinyl "Brickette" doll, 1961 by the Vogue Doll Co., character girl has green flirty/sleep eyes, bright orange hair and freckles. Comes with fashion sunglasses. Overall condition fine.

$80-$100

Other Dolls

5" rubber jointed baby, marked "Made in Occupied Japan," in a metal Wyandotte buggy, marked "Made in USA."

$100+/pair

6" bride and groom, chalk-like plastic (carnival dolls?), painted side-glancing eyes, both in original outfits.

$50-$100/pair

9" Charlie Brown and Lucy dolls, molded and painted vinyl, marked "United Features Syndicate," circa 1970s.

$80+/pair

10" Topo Gigio mouse doll, vinyl, 1960s, marked on foot, "Roydes of Florida, Creative Vinyl Prod., Royalty Inc." (Created by Maria Perego, the Italian mouse Topo Gigio appeared on "The Ed Sullivan Show" 92 times from 1963 until the show's last broadcast in 1971.)

$40+

Two 11" Gerber Baby dolls, jointed rubber bodies (beginning to deteriorate), marked "Gerber Product Co. Manufactured by Sun Rubber Co.", redressed (?).

$50+/pair

Two rubber dolls: 12" white, made by Sun Rubber Co., $25+; 11" black "Amos Sandra," marked "Sunruco Viceroy Drink & Wet Doll."

$100+

12" Popeye and Olive Oyl, vinyl heads, cloth plush bodies, $75+ each; shown with Wimpy and Sweet Pea hand puppets, vinyl faces, fair condition.

$30+ each

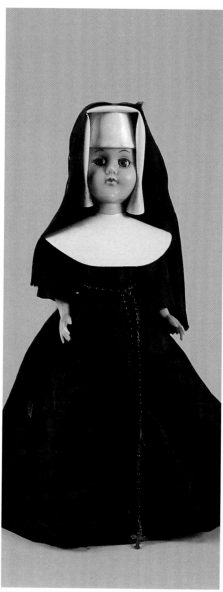

13" unmarked hard plastic doll in original nun garb, blue sleep eyes.

$50+

Two 13" Buddy Lee dolls, hard plastic, wearing original cowboy outfits and hats. (Originally a 1920s advertising promotion for Dayton's Department Stores in Minneapolis, Buddy Lees were made in hard plastic beginning in 1949. Production of the dolls halted in the 1960s. There are also several look-alikes.)

$150+ each

13 1/2" Mickey and Minnie Mouse, marked on shoes "No. 3227, Gund," vinyl faces and hands, hard stuffed cloth bodies.

$250+/pair

14 1/2" Mickey Mouse and 10" Mickey Mouse, vinyl faces, plastic ears, plush bodies, stuffed with foam, tagged "Mickey Mouse, Walt Disney Productions, Gund Mfg."

$150+/pair

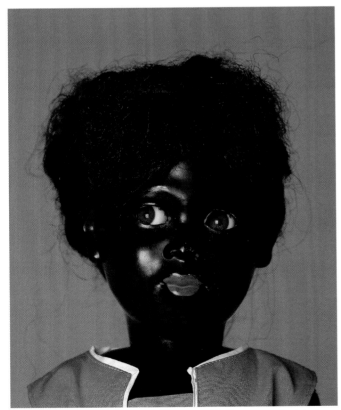

17" English black hard-plastic girl. Character with flirty eyes and original dress. Wig appears to be original. Minute scuff on cheek and fingertips.

$100-$150

18" Wanda Walker made by Advance Doll Co., hard plastic, wind-up key under dress, blue sleep eyes, blonde hair, metal feet.

$75+

21" Clown Willie, marked "Baby Barry Toy, NYC", vinyl face, cloth body, original clothing.

$80+

22" vinyl Snow White, marked on head "Disney Productions," sleep eyes, original yellow and blue dress, red cape; 8" vinyl Seven Dwarves, marked with names on feet.

$200/set

22" Jerry Mahoney ventriloquist doll, vinyl head and hands, cloth body, marked "1967 Juro Nov. Inc. Co.," all original.

$75+

22" hard plastic doll, unmarked, jointed body, blue sleep eyes, closed mouth. Attire may be original.

$150-$200

23" Mary Hartline doll (named for the star of the "Super Circus" TV show), hard plastic, blonde curly hair, sleep eyes, closed mouth, jointed body, dressed in a copy of original majorette uniform, white boots.

$250-$275

24" hard plastic doll, lady-type body, blue sleep eyes, dark brown hair, wearing original red dress and high-heeled shoes.

$250+

Wood Dolls

Figures carved from wood are some of the oldest and most sought-after of all dolls. From fragile 17th century examples to contemporary artist creations, such dolls represent a special collecting challenge.

Prone to damage because of the expansion and contraction of the wood, painted surfaces are often crazed and crackled, and professional restoration can be expensive, if available at all.

While many vintage dolls employed some wood in their construction, this section focuses on dolls with carved and shaped wooden heads, and bodies constructed with significant wooden components.

Some guidelines to collecting categories include:

English

William and Mary: 1680-1720; carved, one-piece head and torso with distinctive facial expression; human hair or flax nailed to head for wig; well painted almond-shaped eyes with little detail; single-stroke brows extend from curve of nose and end at outer corner of eye; well-defined nose, mouth, ears, and rosy cheeks; limbs attached by various pinning and jointing methods; upper arms usually made of bound linen; carved wooden lower arms and hands; separate fingers and thumbs; often detailed fingernails; upper and lower legs, usually wooden with well-carved toes; entire body covered with gesso base layer, delicately painted with flesh color and varnished; dressed in fashionable period costume; unmarked.

Queen Anne: 1700-1750; more stylized, less individual appearance; a high level of craftsmanship; one-piece head and body; linen upper arms nailed to shoulders; shaped bosom, narrow waist; rounded fingers with fingernails; hips curved on each side to accommodate pegged tongue-and-groove joints; human hair or flax wig nailed to head; oval, almost egg-shaped head; bulbous

glass or painted oval eyes; brows and lashes indicated by a series of dots; well-defined nose and ears; closed mouth; rosy cheeks; entire body covered with gesso base layer; painted, pale flesh color and varnished; dressed in fashionable period costume; unmarked.

Georgian: 1750-1800; one-piece carved head and body; somewhat rounded head; torso has rounded chest, narrow waist, squared hips, and flat back; upper arms of linen stitched to torso through hole drilled in shoulders; lower arms and hands carved with separate flat fingers and thumbs, and covered in kid with fingers exposed; legs carved to fit into carved slots of hips with pegged tongue-and-groove joints; human hair or flax wig nailed to head; well-defined nose and mouth; inserted lozenge-shaped glass eyes; brows and lashes indicated by a series of dots; closed, small mouth; entire body covered with gesso base layer; painted, pale flesh color and varnished; dressed in fashionable period costume; unmarked.

Early 19th Century: 1800-1840; carved, one-piece head and torso; base of torso forms a point; arms attached to body with piece of linen; legs carved to fit against either side of pointed torso; then pegged with one single peg going first through one leg, then torso, and into other leg; stitched flax or human hair wig glued to head; well painted facial features; painted, oversized, oval-shaped eyes; single-stroke brows; no ears; closed mouth; dark, rosy cheeks; upper body and lower limbs covered with gesso layer; painted a flesh color and varnished; typically dressed in gown much longer than legs, often with matching bonnet; unmarked.

German

Early to Mid-19th Century: 1810–1840; carved, one-piece head and torso; often with high or Empire waist; all wooden arms; tongue-and-groove joints applied to shoulders and elbows, allowing easy mobility. Carved and painted hair, at times in elaborate styles, with curls around the face and the addition of a hair comb carved into the back of the head. (Collectors often speak of "yellow tuck comb" when referring to this characteristic.) The nose was most often a wedge inserted into the face and heavily painted, somewhat sharp in appearance. Earrings were common as were closed mouths. No gesso base layer, with heavy paint applied directly to the wood and only on exposed areas. Fashionably dressed in period costume. Unmarked.

Later 19th Century: 1840–1900; carved, one-piece head and torso; similar to the Early to Mid-19th Century doll in body configuration and facial features; painting may be crude; no hair comb, and the hair styles tend to be less elaborate with perhaps only a bun or carved side curls; fashionably dressed in period costumes; unmarked.

Bohemian Wooden Doll: turned wooden head; kid joins arms and legs to carved, red-painted torso; small waist; spoon-like hands; carved nose; painted facial features; appropriately dressed; unmarked.

Late 19th Century: carved wooden shoulder head and limbs; cloth body; simple, carved hair style; painted eyes; closed mouth; appropriately dressed; unmarked.

Peg Wooden or Dutch Wooden: after 1900; simple construction; jointed and fastened with wooden pegs; sharp, little carved noses, protruding from simple, round faces; painted, black hair; painted facial feature; stick-type limbs; spoon-like hands; painted white lower legs; black shoes; appropriately dressed; unmarked.

Bébé Tout en Bois: (dolls all of wood); 1900–1914; manufactured by F. M. Schilling, its subsidiary Rudolf Schneider, and possibly others. Well carved head, resembling dolly-faced or character baby; fully jointed wooden or cloth body with wooden arms and legs; good wig; glass eyes; painted brows and lashes; open mouth with teeth; appropriately dressed; typically marked with the trademark "Angle," a sticker in three languages "Tout Bois, Holz, All Wood," or unmarked.

Swiss

Early 1900s: socket head or shoulder head; detailed facial carving; all wood or cloth body with wooden limbs; carved and painted hair, often with intricate detailing; painted eyes with tiny lines going through iris to look like threading, usually with reflective white dot in middle; closed mouth; often wearing regional costumes; typically stamped on back of leg, "Made in Switzerland," unmarked, or wrist tag only.

Wooden Dolls, makers unknown

Two 12" wooden penny dolls, all hand-carved with painted black hair, one doll dressed as a peddler.

$100+ each

13" Queen Anne-type wooden doll. Dressed in old print fabric and has pupil-less brown glass eyes. Head has been professionally restored and it is believed that arms are also replacements.

$700-$900

15" black carved wooden lady holding a black baby. Caricature of the black "mammy" sitting in a rocker holding her child. Body is jointed and completely carved in an intricate fashion. Baby is black-painted bisque. Fine original condition.

$400-$500

16" French court doll. Wood with inset glass pupil-less eyes. Costume of silk and gold brocade has deteriorated with age, but doll is in all original untouched condition.

$800-$1,000

17" English wood William & Mary doll. From the late 17th century and appears to be in all original, untouched condition. Finely molded facial details including elaborately carved ears and painted eyes, mouth and cheeks. Fingers are well defined and carved (damage to three fingers on right hand). Wooden legs are covered in green silk, with leather shoes. Chartreuse silk dress covers a multi-colored linen skirt with an aqua blue blouse, gauze apron and a bonnet. Original skull cap intact but majority of hair is missing. Two scuffs to doll's left cheek.

$45,000-$50,000

17" wood French court doll. Carved wood with a jointed body and molded and carved hair. In original untouched condition. Wooden torso with legs (painted socks and shoes) connected at the hip, a carved bust and sex organs, and well-detailed hands connected at the elbow. Wearing period print costume that is somewhat frail, and a lace and satin bonnet attached by ribbon through hairdo. Overall very good. Crazing to original paint finish on all wood painted surfaces. Rare.

$5,000-$6,000

Two 18" hand-carved crèche figures, angel and shepherd, probably Mexican in origin.

$200+ each

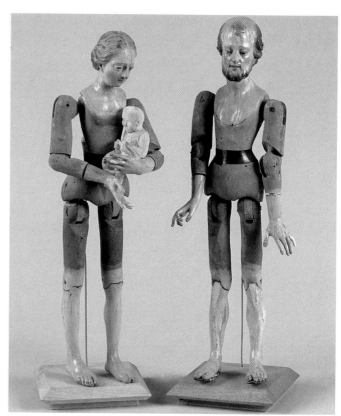

Two 18" hand-carved crèche figures, Mary (holding infant) and Joseph, painted, probably Italian.

$500-$1,000 each

19" Queen Anne-type wooden doll. With brown pupil-less faceted glass eyes, carved facial details, molded breastplate, wooden arms and jointed wooden legs. Undergarment is a cotton print that is covered by a quilted chartreuse leaded satin skirt which is in turn covered by an aqua leaded satin dress and topped with a gauze coverlet that is enhanced with embroidery. Brown human hair wig (replaced) and lace bonnet with silk pink and silver brocade ribbon. Small amount of touch-up to face.

$3,800-$4,200

23" Queen Anne-type wooden doll. Large glass-eyes, wooden torso with wooden lower legs jointed at the hip. The arms are cloth and probably were replaced. Brown human hair wig and replica silk gown. Overall fair with much paint loss to chin and elsewhere on face.

$800-$900

26" Queen Anne-type wooden doll. Eighteenth-century, with inset glass pupil-less eyes, fine facial carving, and molded bust. Paint restoration to the face as well as replaced or repainted limbs. Dressed in a white cotton dress with early metal embroidered silk hat.

$2,500-$3,000

Pair of French "tout en bois" (all wood) babies. Both have brown glass eyes, one with painted hair, and one with mohair. Doll with mohair wig has a split at the right eye. Both have some flaking to bodies.

$350-$450/pair

Shadow box display of early wooden dolls. According to paper on rear of shadow box, these carved wooden "Peg Dolls" are probably of German manufacture, circa 1840s. Thirteen "woodens," approximately 1" to 4" tall. Case size approximately 8 1/2" by 12" by 3". It appears that there has been paint restoration to many of the dolls.

$450-$550/set

Door of Hope Dolls, 1901 to 1949

These dolls were made in Shanghai and Canton, China, at a Protestant mission called the Door of Hope, established to rescue and educate destitute children and slave girls.

At the Door of Hope Mission, the girls were taught needlework, embroidery, knitting, and other skills used to make the doll clothing. The head, hands, and arms to the elbow were carved of pear wood. The smooth wood was not painted or varnished. The hair, eyes, and lips were painted. A few of the dolls had fancy buns or flowers carved into their heads. Most have hands with rounded palms and separate thumbs, although some have been found with cloth stub hands. Cloth bodies were stuffed with raw cotton donated to the mission by local textile factories. The elaborate handmade costumes are exact copies of clothing worn by the Chinese people. Dolls were unmarked, or labeled "Made in China."

Kindergarten Kid
6" Door of Hope Chinese "kindergarten kid." Intricately carved wood with fancy silk clothing and carved wooden arms. Fine original condition.
$2,800-$3,200

Small Child
7 1/4" Door of Hope Chinese small girl. Intricately carved wood with fancy silk outfit and carved wooden arms. Fine original condition.
$3,300-$3,600

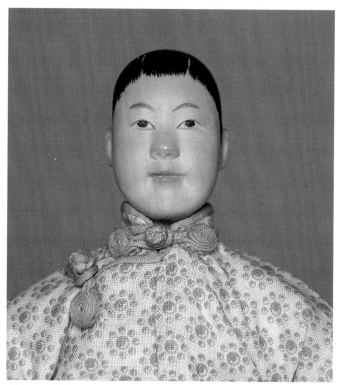

Chinese Schoolgirl
8" Door of Hope Chinese schoolgirl. Intricately carved wood with cotton print outfit with fancy carved braid with queue at base and carved wooden arms. Slight soiling to outfit.
$1,200-$1,500

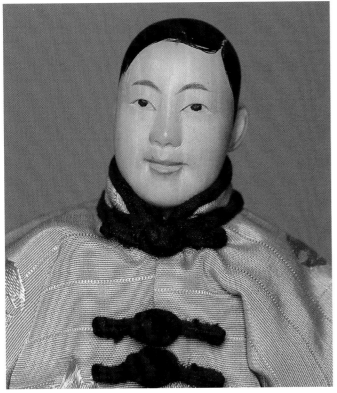

Chinese Youth
8 1/4" Door of Hope Chinese youth. Intricately carved wood with fancy silk clothing and carved wooden arms. Fine original condition.

$900-$1,200

School Boy
8 1/2" Door of Hope Chinese "school boy." Intricately carved wood with polished cotton outfit and hat and carved wooden arms. Some fading and soiling to front of outfit.

$1,000-$1,300

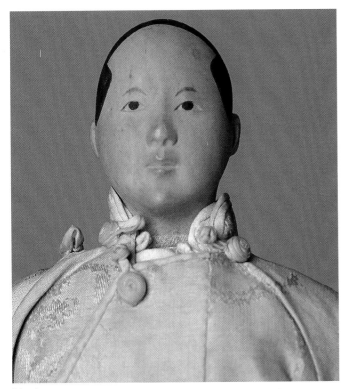

Mother
10 3/4" Door of Hope Chinese mother. Intricately carved wood with fancy bun at back of head, fancy silk outfit and carved wooden arms. Slight soiling to outfit.

$300-$400

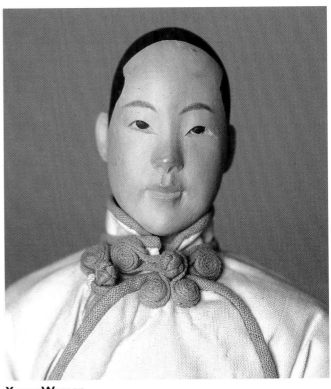

Young Woman
11" Door of Hope Chinese young woman. Intricately carved wood with fancy bun at back of head, polished cotton outfit and carved wooden arms. Soiling and fading to outfit.

$1,000-$1,300

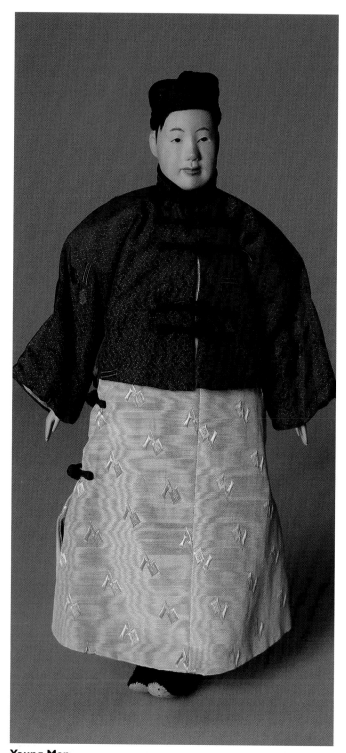

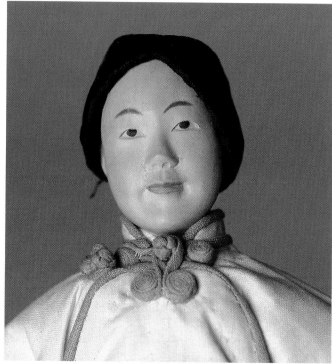

Amah
11" Door of Hope Chinese "amah." Intricately carved wood with polished cotton clothing, wearing an unusual velvet headpiece (open at back but covering ears and exposing the back of head, which depicts a fancy bun) and carved wooden arms. Slight soiling to clothes.

$800-$900

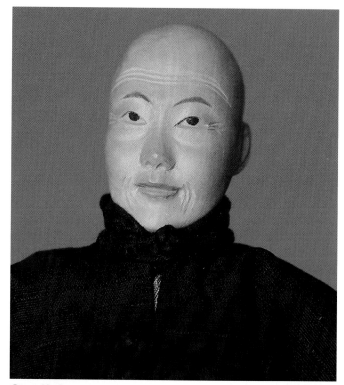

Young Man
11" Door of Hope Chinese young man. Intricately carved wood with fancy silk outfit and hat with wooden arms. Fine original condition.

$1,600-$2,000

Grandfather
11" Door of Hope Chinese grandfather. Intricately carved wood, with facial detail, with silk outfit and hat, and carved wooden arms. Significant fading to front of outfit.

$1,600-$2,000

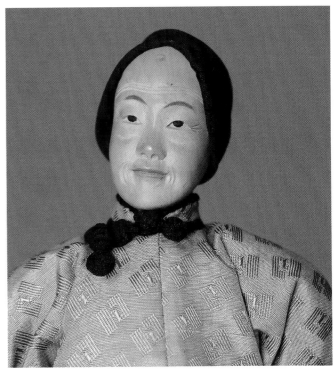

Grandmother

11" Door of Hope Chinese grandmother. Intricately carved wood, with facial detail, with silk outfit and headpiece (open at back but covering ears & exposing the back of head, which depicts a bun and thinning hair) and carved wooden arms. Significant fading to front of jacket.

$1,800-$2,200

Manchu Woman

11" Door of Hope "Manchu Woman." Intricately carved wood with elaborately carved headpiece, silk clothing and carved wooden arms, legs, and shoes. Fine original condition.

$7,500-$8,500

Farmer

11" Door of Hope Chinese male farmer. Intricately carved wood with cotton and straw outfit with wooden arms and feet. Fine original condition.

$2,500-$3,000

Young Man
11 1/4" Door of Hope Chinese young man. Intricately carved wood with silk and polished cotton outfit with carved wooden arms. Significant fading to cotton outfit and scuffs and wear to head.

$900-$1,200

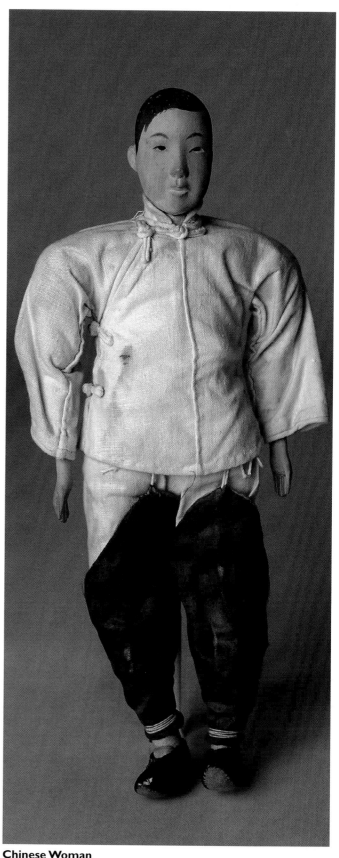

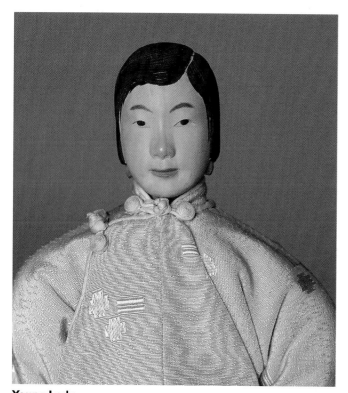

Young Lady
11 1/4" Door of Hope Chinese young lady. Intricately carved wood, with facial detail and finely carved hair, with silk outfit and carved wooden arms. Some fading to front of outfit where tag was once pinned.

$2,000-$2,500

Chinese Woman
11 1/4 Door of Hope Chinese woman. Intricately carved wood (hair swirled into bun at rear of head), fancy silk clothing, fancy beaded headdress and carved wooden arms. Fine original condition.

$1,000-$1,400

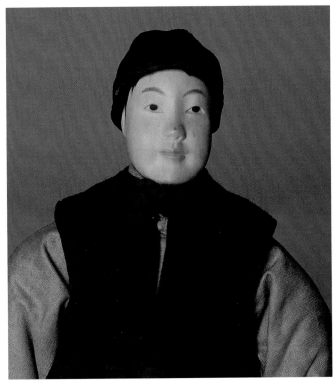

Table Boy
11 1/2" Door of Hope Chinese "table boy." Intricately carved wood with fancy silk clothing and carved wooden arms. Slight soiling and fading to lavender outfit.

$1,200-$1,600

Bride
11 1/2" Door of Hope Chinese bride. Intricately carved wood with highly detailed silk outfit with flowers and fancy headdress, and carved wooden arms. Fine original condition.

$1,200-$1,600

Bridegroom
11 1/2" Door of Hope bridegroom. Intricately carved wood with elaborate plum silk outfit and hat with and carved wooden arms. Fine original condition.

$1,200-$1,600

Priest
11 1/2" Door of Hope Chinese priest. Intricately carved wood with olive green muslin outfit and carved wooden arms. Fine original condition.
$2,900-$3,300

Mourner
11 1/2" Door of Hope Chinese male mourner. Intricately carved wood with fancy muslin and burlap clothing including hat, and carved wooden arms. Fine original condition.
$1,100-$1,500

Policeman
12" Door of Hope Chinese policeman. Intricately carved wood with fancy cotton outfit with silk hat and carved wooden arms. Fine original condition.
$2,800-$3,300

A. Schoenhut & Co., founded 1872

Located in Philadelphia, Albert Schoenhut came from a family of German toy makers. He came to the U.S. at the age of 17, and at 22 established his own toy factory. Schoenhut's first toy was a piano.

The Humpty Dumpty Circus, introduced in 1903, probably included Schoenhut's first attempt at doll making. The ringmaster, lion tamer, lady circus rider, and gentleman and lady acrobats are identified solely by their characteristic painting and costuming. At about this time, Schoenhut introduced the Chinaman, Hobo, Negro Dude, Farmer, Milkmaid, and Max and Mortiz. Rolly-Dollys were patented in 1908, as was Teddy Roosevelt and his "Teddy Adventures in Africa."

In 1909, Schoenhut filed a patent application for his swivel, spring-jointed dolls, but the patent was not granted until 1911. The metal joints had springs that compressed, rather than stretched when pulled, adding to the durability of the doll. In addition to the unique spring joints, the wooden dolls were painted entirely with oil colors. Their solid wood heads came with either mohair wigs or molded hair. The feet are of hardwood with two holes drilled into the soles to enable the doll to be placed on its stand and posed. One hole was drilled at an angle and one straight, allowing the doll to hold its feet in both the tip-toe and flat positions.

Following Albert Schoenhut's death in 1912, he was succeeded by his six sons: Harry, Gustav, Theodore, Albert Jr., William, and Otto. The new directors introduced an infant doll with curved limbs in 1913. It is identified by the © copyright symbol on its head.

The dolly-faced all-wooden dolls produced in 1915 had rounded eyes, advertised as "imitation glass," as opposed to intaglio eyes, and mohair wigs. The dolls came in an accordion-type box with detailed instructions for posing. A round, tin doll stand with pins to accommodate the holes in the feet was included. A series of 19" tall older boy dolls, called "Manikins," commonly dressed as athletes, was also introduced in 1915. Only 1,000 of the male Manikins were produced. The bent-limb baby with split joints at the elbows and knees was also produced for the first time in 1915.

Walking dolls, jointed at the shoulder and hip only, were introduced in 1919. They were the first dolls without foot holes. In 1921, sleep eyes were added to the Schoenhut babies along with the dolly-faced dolls.

Cloth-bodied mama dolls and a less expensive line of dolls with elastic joints were marketed in 1924.

Dolly Face
15" Schoenhut dolly face. Carved wood with molded and painted teeth, blonde mohair wig (replaced) on a jointed wood body. Painted eyes and finely feathered eyebrows and has been redressed. Some paint crazing to cheeks.
$150-$200

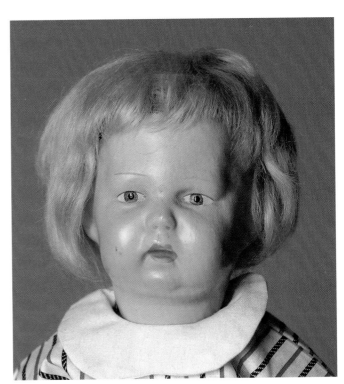

Mama
16" Schoenhut "mama" doll. Blonde mohair wig and blue painted eyes on a cloth body with wood hands and "mama" cry box, wearing new striped romper. Light crazing, original paint, skullcap is original, but mohair has been attached. Crier is in working condition.
$350-$450

Boy

17" Schoenhut boy brown painted eyes, open mouth with painted teeth, jointed wood body, wearing cotton shirt and blue and white striped suit and navy tie. (Shown with all wood jointed Schoenhut elephant.)

$750+(doll only)

Boy

19" Schoenhut boy, brown painted eyes, open mouth with painted teeth, brown wig, jointed wood body, wearing a gray and black striped suit, stockings and leather shoes.

$800+

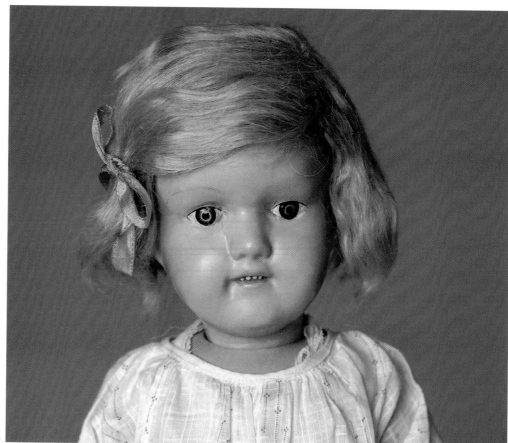

Dolly Face

19" Schoenhut dolly face. Original paint and blonde mohair wig, union suit, and shoes (frail). Wearing a replaced cotton print dress. Brows and lashes are pale and some paint missing to eyes.

$250-$350

Girl
21" Schoenhut girl, paper label, all wood jointed body, open mouth with painted teeth, blonde curly wig, wearing a white cotton dress and leather shoes.

$850+

Girl
21" Schoenhut girl, paper label, all wood jointed body, open mouth with painted teeth, brown braided wig, wearing a checked cotton dress and leather shoes.

$850+

Other Wooden Dolls

11" jointed wood Disney Pinocchio made by Ideal, with "Disney Ideal" label on head; and jointed wood Disney Ferdinand the Bull, marked "Ideal Novelty Toy" on stomach.

$225-$250 each

Other Dolls

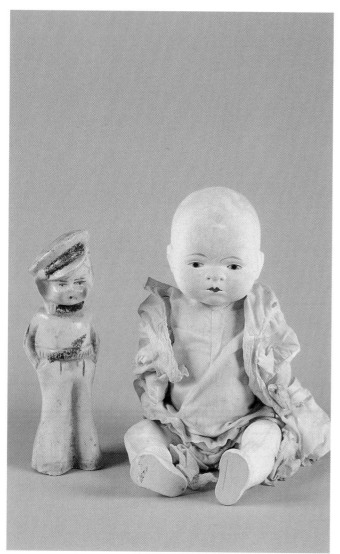

Left, 9" carnival sailor girl.

Right, Bye-Lo Baby in plaster, all jointed, rare.

$25+

$125+

11" carnival Kewpie-style plaster figure, painted suit, brown wig.

$25+

Peddler Dolls

During the late 18th and early 19th centuries, peddler dolls were popular fashion accessories. Frequently created to exhibit a woman's artistic talents, a peddler doll depicted a traveling vendor, and served as a decorating accent, sometimes placed under a glass dome in a prominent location.

Itinerant traders traveled over Europe and the United States, but it was the English peddler doll for which there seemed a special fascination. Women traveled about the countryside selling needles, pins, and other small articles. These women were called "Notion Nannies," and were familiar figures in English country districts.

The weathered and wrinkled dolls made to resemble these travelers were made of cloth, leather, wood, papier-mâché, wax, cork, china, dried apples, and even breadcrumbs. The bodies were usually wooden or cloth-covered wire. The Notion Nannies—with traditional red cape, calico dress gathered to expose a black quilted slip, white apron, and black silk bonnet over a white-laced "mob" cap—were a particular favorite.

Although the majority of vintage peddler dolls were homemade, C. H. White of Portsmouth, England, advertised commercially made dolls. The marbleized paper-cover base and "C. H. White/Milton/Portsmouth" label allows for easy identification.

10" wax peddler doll with wares. With cloth body and a table full of merchandise. Most pieces appear to be original. Large split at forehead continuing down through eye.

$2,500-$3,000

Doll Clothing and Accessories

Most dolls are not complete without the proper clothes and accessories, including dresses, underwear, hats, shoes and socks, even parasols, purses, furniture, and trunks. A casual Internet search turned up more than 120,000 references to everything from gowns for 1840s china-head dolls to the latest baubles worn by Barbie and her friends.

Items listed here were sold at an auction conducted by James D. Julia Inc. of Fairfield, Maine, in the fall of 2003.

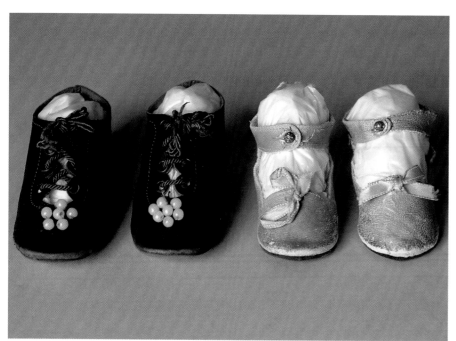

Jumeau and German doll shoes. Marked "Jumeau" (size 9) aqua doll shoes along with a pair of early German doll shoes marked "10" on bottom. 3" and 3 3/4" long, respectively. In good to fine condition. (Pierre Francois Jumeau, Paris, founded about 1842).

$550-$600/set

"A.T." doll shoes. Marked on bottom "A.T." in an oval with "10" stamped into toe. Black strap shoes with rosettes and buckle on top of rosette. 3 1/4" long. Very good original condition. (A. Thuillier, Paris, active 1875-1893)

$1,000-$1,100/pair

Salesman sample hat and pair of doll shoes. French, with label of lion with staff, and a pair of German man's boots in black and taupe oilcloth. Both in excellent condition.

$200-$250/set

2 1/2" all original Golli-Wog perfume bottle. In good original condition with paper label intact. (Also spelled Golliwog and Golliwogg, this caricature of a black minstrel performer was the creation of author Florence Grace Upton, introduced in her 1895 book, The Adventures of Two Dutch Dolls.)

$150-$200

Pair of walnut doll dressers, both with mirrors. Measuring 10" by 6" by 19", and 11" by 4 1/2" by 14". Overall condition is very good, with original finish.

$125-$175/pair

Antique rosewood doll piano. Top opens to show detail of strings. Does not play.

$125-$175

German doll trunk. Domed top with many storage pockets and drawers decorated with paper litho. Some newer clothes, fabric pieces, and antique bedding and pillows. Metal trim loose, handles missing, and some paper wear.

$150-$200

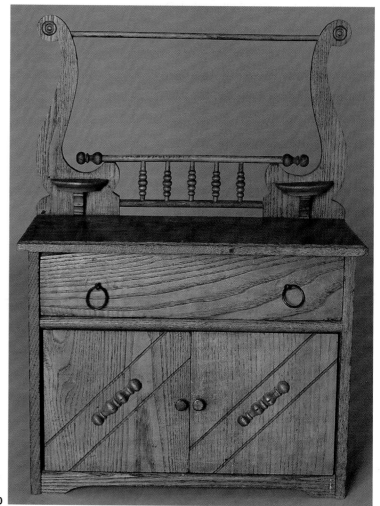

Oak doll washstand. With drawer and doors below. The top has a harp-shaped towel rack with two small shelves attached; 16" by 8" by 22" Overall condition is very good with original finish. There is a chip to the surface of the stand.

$50-$70

Doll Clubs

A casual Internet search turned up more than 350,000 references to doll clubs all over the world, focusing on everything from 18th century automata to 21st century action figures.

A great place to find the right doll club for you is the United Federation of Doll Clubs (U.F.D.C.) at www.ufdc.org.

Headquartered in Kansas City, Mo., the United Federation of Doll Clubs has a doll museum and maintains permanent archives of historical documents relating to dolls. It offers educational events, such as national conventions and regional conferences, and a lending library of slide and video programs. The U.F.D.C.'s official publication, Doll News, is published quarterly.

Another excellent resource for locating other doll enthusiasts—whether collectors, buyers, sellers, or specialists—is Maloney's Antiques & Collectibles Resource Directory and its online counterpart, MaloneysOnline.com. The directory lists 17,000 resources to assist in the location, study and authentication, replacement, repair, valuation, or buying and selling of more than 2,900 categories of antiques, collectibles, and other types of personal property.

Collectors can locate clubs or subscribe to specialty publications to learn more about their areas of interest.

Since its debut, Maloney's Antiques & Collectibles Resource Directory has been hailed as the "...best one-volume research tool in print." (Gannett News Service) and as a Best Reference Book (Library Journal).

Resources listed in Maloney's include:
* Buyers
* Collector Reference Book Sources
* Collectors
* Dealers
* Experts
* General Line and Specialty Auction Services
* Internet Resources
* Manufacturers and Distributors of Modern Collectibles
* Matching Services for China/Flatware/Crystal
* Overseas Antiques Tour Guides
* Regional Guides to Antiques Shops and Flea Markets
* Repair, Restoration, and Conservation Specialists
* Reproduction Sources
* Specialty Collector Clubs
* Specialty Museums and Library Collections
* Specialty Periodicals
* Suppliers of Parts
* Trained Appraisers

Dollhouses

There was a time when most little girls (and a few boys) spent hours moving tiny people around the rooms of treasured dollhouses. Often homemade, the familiar structures with three outer walls and one open side taught lessons in social interaction, interior decorating, and … pure fun, for the most part.

Petite dolls made for Victorian-era dollhouses originated in the 1880s. Most dollhouses included a wife, husband, several children, two or three maids, a butler, and at least a few visiting friends. Early bisque dollhouse dolls were made in Germany. They are often unmarked or marked with a number or letter only.

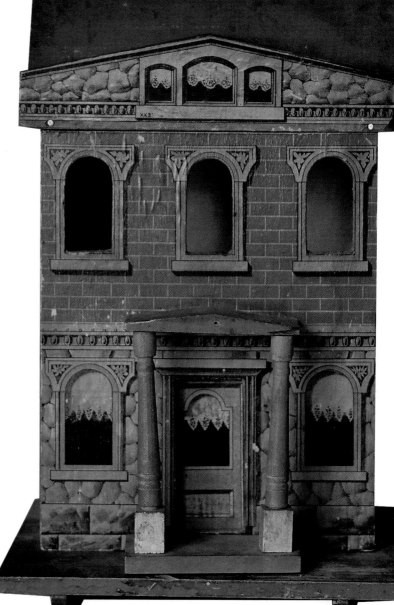

Whitney Reed dollhouse, with stone and brick façade. The front opens to reveal two rooms inside. Minor paper flaking throughout. House probably had glass windows on second floor, which are now lacking. Small chip to wood on porch covering, otherwise overall condition is very good. 7 1/2" by 6 1/2" by 11"

$550-$600

Books about Dollhouses and Furnishings

A Beginners' Guide to the Dolls' House Hobby by Jean Nisbett

Antique and Collectible Dollhouses and Their Furnishings by Dian Zillner, Patty Cooper

Barbie Doll Structure and Furniture by Marl B. Davidson

Celtic, Medieval and Tudor Wall Hangings in 1/12 Scale Needlepoint by Sandra Whitehead

Decorate A Doll's House by Michal Morse

Dollhouse Decor: Creating Soft Furnishings in 1/12 Scale by Nick Forder, Esther Forder

Dollhouse Furnishings for the Bedroom and Bath by Shep Stadtman

Dollhouse Living by Beauregard Houston-Montgomery, Wendy Goodman (Introduction)

Dolls' House Accessories, Fixtures & Fittings by Andrea Barham

Doll's House by Rumer Godden, Tasha Tudor (Illustrator)

Easy-To-Make Dollhouse Quilts (Dover Needlework Series) by Janet Wickell

Furnished Dollhouses, 1880s-1980s by Dian Zillner

Make and Clothe Your Own Dollhouse Dolls by Ellen Bedington

Miniature Embroidery for the Victorian Dolls' House by Pamela Warner

Queen Mary's Dolls' House by Mary Stewart-Wilson, David Cripps

Tasha Tudor's Dollhouse: A Lifetime in Miniature by Harry Davis, Jay Paul

The Art of Making Miniature Millinery by M. Dalton King, Pat Henry, Timothy J. Alberts

The Art of Tasha Tudor by Harry Davis, Tasha Tudor (Illustrator)

The Art of the Miniature: Small Worlds and How to Make Them by Jane Freeman, Roger Rosenblatt

The Decorated Doll House: How to Design and Create Miniature Interiors by Jessica Ridley

The Dollhouse Book by Stephanie Finnegan

The Dollhouse Sourcebook by Caroline Clifton-Mogg, Nick Nicholson (Photographer)

The Dollhouse Sourcebook from Abbeville Press, Inc.

The Dolls' House Shopkeeper by Lionel Barnard, Ann Barnard

The Pistner House ... A Master In Miniature by Patricia Pistner, James Lilliefors

Tomart's Price Guide to Tin Litho Doll Houses and Plastic Doll House Furniture by Mary O. Brett, et al.

Victorian Dollhouse Wallpapers by Warren Katzenbach

Vivien Greene's Doll's Houses: The Complete Rotunda Collection by Vivien Greene, Margaret Towner

Within the Fairy Castle: Colleen Moore's Doll House at the Museum of Science and Industry, Chicago, by Colleen Moore, et al

Doll Repair, Restoration and Replacement Parts

Professional restoration of doll heads, bodies, and limbs can turn worn and damaged figures into like-new examples of the doll maker's art, whether they are 19th century European bisque or 20th century plastic.

The following images are courtesy of Graves Doll Studio, Rochester, Minn., (507) 753-2741, kvgraves@rconnect.com. Examples of the Graves Studio's work, which includes handmade cloth and kid bodies, parts, heads and kits, can also be seen at http://members.ebay.com/aboutme/kmgtoy/.

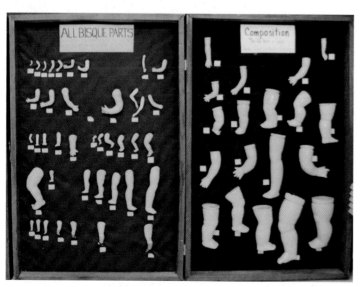

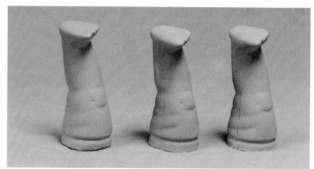

Replacement composition legs, 6 1/2" long, shown finished (left), semi-finished (center), and unfinished.

Replacement porcelain straight-wrist forearms, 4" long, shown with china finish (left), flesh finish (center), and Parian finish.

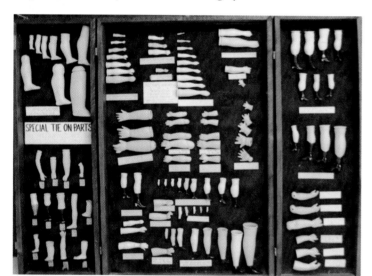

Replacement porcelain legs with molded boot feet, 3 1/2" long, shown with china finish (left), flesh finish (center), and Parian finish.

Doll limbs in dozens of shapes and sizes are on display at Graves Doll Studio.

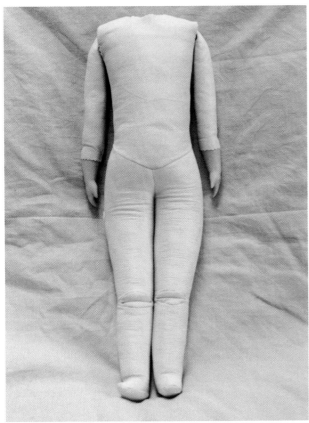

Handmade replacement kid body with bisque forearms, jointed at the shoulders, hips and knees, 22" long.

Hard-plastic doll heads from the late 1940s and early 1950s in various sizes have been cleaned and polished, ready for new bodies.

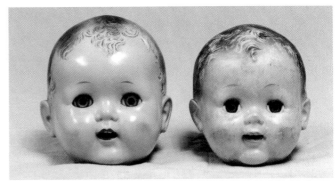

Two hard-plastic doll heads: left, after cleaning; right, before cleaning with years of grime, mold, and wear. Cleaning of heads ranges in price from $15 to $25.

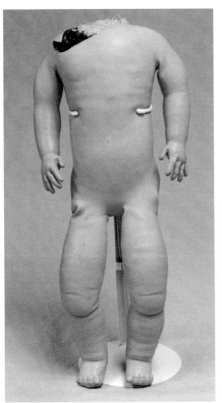

Circa 1950 doll body, 18" tall, covered in Magic Skin, a soft latex material usually filled with shredded cloth and excelsior, with typical cracking and deterioration around neck, otherwise good condition.

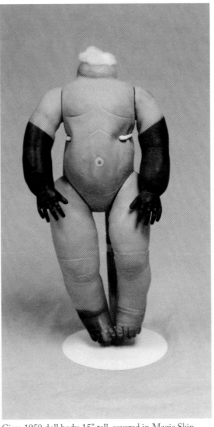

Circa 1950 doll body, 15" tall, covered in Magic Skin, showing common discoloration of limbs.

Circa 1950 doll, 24 1/2" tall, with Magic Skin limbs and cloth body (can be salvaged), and hard-plastic head with eyes that need resetting. Note color difference between hard-plastic head and limbs.

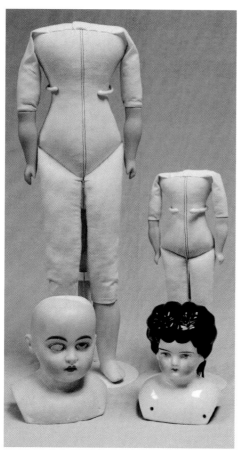

Left, 19" new replacement muslin doll body with straight wrists and lower limbs in flesh bisque ($50-$60), and a vintage bisque shoulder head (probably by Cuno and Otto Dressel, circa 1910), awaiting replacement leather body.

Right, 11" new replacement muslin body with china arms and lower limbs with molded boots ($25-$30), and a German china shoulder head with molded hair, circa 1890.

Left, vintage bisque shoulder head (probably by Cuno and Otto Dressel, circa 1910), 5 3/4" tall, awaiting replacement leather body.

Right, a new bisque head ready for wig and eyes, 4 3/4" tall. New bisque heads can be used as replacements on old leather bodies.

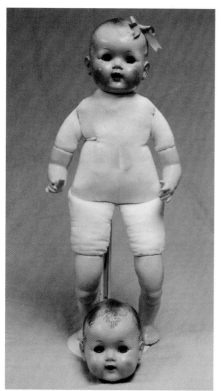

Doll with vintage hard-plastic head (possibly by Ideal, 1950s) with new muslin body and cast limbs, ready for dressing. (Also shown is the same head with color variation and more wear.) Complete restoration for this doll ranges from $100 to $125.

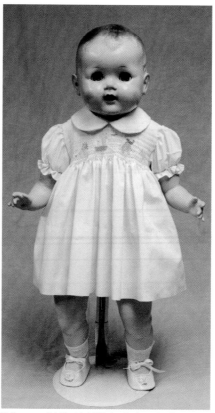

Fully restored doll with 1950s hard-plastic head, new body and limbs, dressed in 1950s baby clothes, new shoes and socks. $175-$200

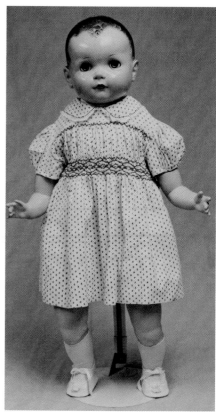

Fully restored Baby Coos, 28 1/2" tall, made by Ideal from 1948 to 1952, wearing old baby clothes and new socks and shoes.

All original Baby Coos, 26 1/2" tall, made by Ideal from 1948 to 1952, wearing original clothes. Note grime on hands; this is often best left untouched to avoid damage.

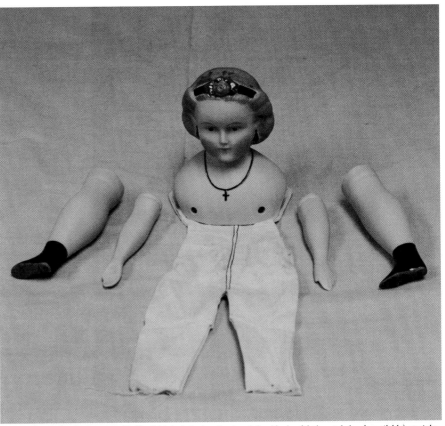

New doll kit (15" tall when assembled), which includes hand-painted shoulder head (other style heads available), straight-wrist forearms, legs with molded shoe feet, and muslin body ready to be filled. $40

Replica of a Gibson Girl doll (the original is circa 1910), 18 1/2" tall, with handmade mohair wig, showing component parts, and dressed in period-style wedding dress. This doll is made with a hollow tube in the body to accept a stand rod.

"Antie Clare's" Doll Hospital & Shop
Doll Repair ... Antique to Modern
2543 Seppala Blvd.
North St. Paul, MN 55109
Phone: (651) 770-7522
Fax: (651) 770-7517
www.antieclares.com
Email: clare@antieclares.com

Since 1970, Antie Clare's Doll Hospital & Shop has done thousands of restorations on dolls, bears, and figurines. Antie Clare's carries wigs, stands, criers, shoes, stockings, dresses, and other accessories. Owner Clare Erickson also gives presentations for conventions, historical societies, doll clubs, mother-daughter banquets, and Christian women's groups. The business also buys and sells dolls.

A counter at Antie Clare's displays vintage dolls, mostly redressed, and accessories.

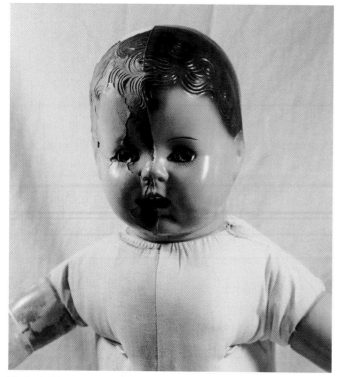

The head of this composition doll had badly deteriorated before restorers at Antie Clare's started to work on it. The business uses this doll to show the kinds of restorations that are possible.

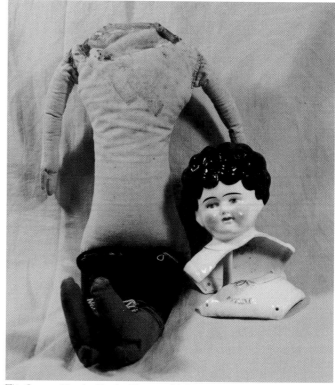

This German china shoulder-head "pet name" doll has a broken shoulder plate and badly worn body. Both can be completely restored.

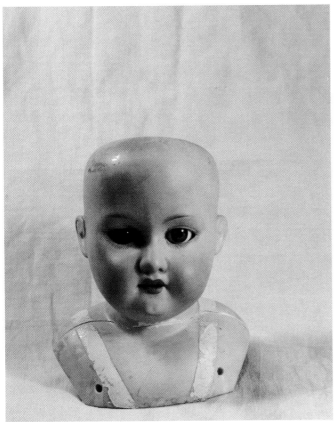

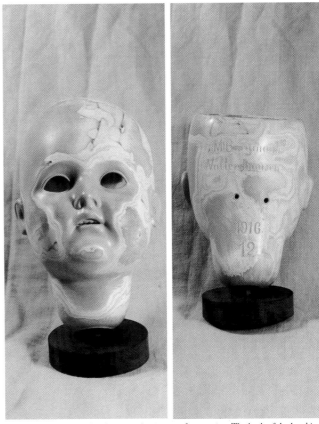

An owner of this German bisque shoulder head used masking tape to temporarily fix the shoulder plate that had split at the base of the neck.

This bisque socket head is shown in the process of restoration. The back of the head is marked, "CM Bergmann – Waltershausen – 1916 – 12."

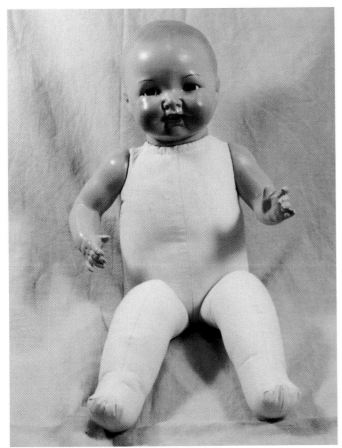

A completely restored doll: 21", composition head and arms, and cloth body and legs, marked "Madame Hendren, Made in USA" (a trademark used by Averill Manufacturing Co., New York, active 1913-1965). Restoration took about 12 months. Restored value is about $400.

Selected Doll Bibliography

200 Years of Dolls, 2nd Edition by Dawn Herlocher

Advertising Character Collectibles: An Identification & Value Guide by Warren Dotz

African and Asian Costumed Dolls Price Guide by Polly Judd, Pam Judd

Alexander Dolls Collector's Price Guide by A. Glenn Mandeville

Americas, Australia, & Pacific Islands Costumed Dolls: Price Guide by Polly Judd, Pam Judd

Antique Trader® Antiques & Collectibles Price Guide™ 2004, Edited by Kyle Husfloen

Antique Trader® Doll Makers & Marks A Guide to Identification by Dawn Herlocher

Barbie: Her Life & Times and the New Theater of Fashion by Billy Boy

Barbie Doll Collector's Handbook by A. Glenn Mandeville, et al.

Barbie the First 30 Years 1959 Through 1989: An Identification and Value Guide by Stefanie Deutsch

Barbie: The Icon, the Image, the Ideal: An Analytical Interpretation of the Barbie Doll in Popular Culture by Kristin Noelle Weissman

Bobbing Head Dolls 1960-2000 by Tim Hunter by John Axe

Collecting Antique Dolls: Fashion Dolls, Automata, Doll Curiosities, Exclusive Dolls by Lydia Richter, Joachim F. Richter (Contributor) Carolyn Cook

Collectors Encyclopedia of American Composition Dolls: 1900-1950: Identification and Values by Ursula R. Mertz

Collector's Encyclopedia of Vogue Dolls: Identification and Values by Judith Izen, Carol Stover

Collectors Guide to Ideal Dolls Identification and Values: (2nd Ed) by Judith Izen

Compo Dolls 1928-1955 Identification and Price Guide by Polly Judd, Pam Judd (Contributor)

Doll Values Antique to Modern by Patsy Moyer

Dolls and Accessories of the 1950s by Dian Zillner

Dolls Are't Just for Kids, The Ultimate Guide for Doll Lovers by Kathrine Peterson, Fannie Roach Palmer

Effanbee A Collector's Encyclopedia 1949 - Present (Revised Edition)

Free Stuff for Doll Lovers on the Internet by Judy Heim, Gloria Hansen, Judith Heim

Ginny, America's Sweetheart by A. Glenn Mandeville

Insider's Guide to China Doll Collecting: Buying, Selling & Collecting Tips by Jan Foulke, Howard Foulke (Photographer)

Insider's Guide to Doll Buying & Selling : Antique to Modern, by Jan Foulke, Howard Foulke

Insider's Guide to German 'Dolly' Collecting: Girl Bisque Dolls: Buying, Selling & Collecting Tips by Jan Foulke, Howard Foulke (Photographer)

Kestner, King of Dollmakers by Jan Foulke, Howard Foulke (Photographer)

Legendary Dolls of Madame Alexander by Cynthia Gaskill

Madame Alexander Dolls, 1965-1990 by Patricia R. Smith

Madame Alexander Dolls, An American Legend by Stephanie Finnegan, Walter Pfeiffer (Photographer)

Madame Alexander: Collector's Dolls Price Guide by Linda Crowsey

Made to Play House : Dolls and the Commercialization of American Girlhood, 1830-1930 by Miriam Formanek-Brunell

Modern Collectible Dolls: Identification and Value Guide by Patsy Moyer

Modern Doll Rarities by Carla Marie Cross

Nancy Ann Storybook Dolls by Marjorie Miller

Sew the Essential Wardrobe for 18-Inch Dolls by Joan Hinds & Jean Becker

Simon & Halbig Dolls: The Artful Aspect by Jan Foulke

Soul Mate Dolls by Noreen Crone-Findlay

Storytelling with Dolls by Elinor Peace Bailey and Noreen Crone-Findlay

The Blue Book of Dolls & Values (1999) by Jan Foulke

The Ginny Doll Encyclopedia by Sue Nettleingham-Roberts, Dorothy Bunker

The Ultimate Barbie© Doll Book by Marcie Melillo

Toys A to Z A Guide and Dictionary for Collectors, Antique Dealers and Enthusiasts by Mark Rich

Books on Doll and Textile Repair and Restoration

Care & Repair of Antique & Modern Dolls by Faith Eaton.

Care of Collections (Leicester Readers in Museum Studies) by Simon Knell (Editor).

Care of Favorite Dolls: Antique Bisque Conservation by Mary Caruso.

Chemical Principles of Textile Conservation (Butterworth-Heinemann Series in Conservation and Museology) by Agnes Timar-Balazsy, Dinah Eastop.

Complete Composition Repair by LaVonne Lutterman.

Conservation Concerns: A Guide for Collectors and Curators by Konstanze Bachmann (Editor), Dianne Pilgrim.

How to Make & Repair Leather Doll Bodies by LaVonne Lutterman.

How to Repair & Restore Dolls by Barbara Kovel.

How to Repair and Dress Dolls by Ruth Freeman.

How to Repair and Dress Old Dolls by Audrey Johnson.

How to Repair Pull-string Talking Toys: Step by Step : Instructions, Drawings, Photographs by Joseph A. Johnson.

Preserving Textiles: A Guide for the Nonspecialist by Harold F. Mailand, et al

Rescuing Vintage Textiles by Mary Beth Temple. Paperback

Restoring Dolls: A Practical Guide by Doreen Perry

Science for Conservators: Cleaning (Heritage: Care-Preservation-Management Programme) by Museums and Galleries Commission Conservation Unit.

The Doll Hospital Directory by Marlene Alperin-Hochman (Editor), et al.

The Handbook of Doll Repair and Restoration by Marty Westfall.

The Textile Conservator's Manual (Butterworth-Heinemann Series in Conservation and Museology) by Sheila Landi.

Your Vintage Keepsake: A CSA Guide to Costume Storage and Display by Margaret T. Ordonez.

Glossary

All Bisque — The entire body and head produced in bisque. Usually under 12" tall; made in France and Germany from about 1850 to the 1930s.

Applied Ears — Ears that are molded separately and affixed to the head.

Appropriately Dressed — Clothing that fits the time period and doll style.

Articulation — Refers to the jointing of a body.

As Is — Often implies damage; no guarantee is made as to actual condition.

BKW — Bent-knee walker; a walking doll that has a knee joint.

Bare Feet — Bisque or fashion dolls with feet having sculpted features.

Ball-Jointed Body — Doll body of wood-and-composition, jointed at shoulders, elbows, wrists, hips, and knees, allowing movement. Also called "Eight-Ball-Jointed Body."

Bathing Dolls — Bisque or china figurines, ranging in size from a few inches to about 12" long, may be found sitting, reclining, or standing.

Bébé — French dolly-faced doll.

Belton-type — A bald head with one, two or three small holes for attaching wig.

Bent-Limb Baby Body — Five-piece baby body of composition with curved arms and legs, jointed at shoulders and hips.

Biscaloid — Ceramic or composition substance for making dolls; also called imitation bisque.

Bisque — Unglazed porcelain; the medium of choice from the 1850s to the 1930s for dolls produced in France and Germany.

Three smoker boudoir dolls. Two of three with original clothing. Overall condition is poor to fair; some repainting to dolls.

$400-$500/set

Blown Glass Eyes — Hollow eyes of blue, brown, or gray.

Blush — Color applied to the cheeks; also applied to knees and back of hands on some dolls. Check for scratches or "rubs" in the color.

Bottle Mouth — also called a "nurser mouth." Has an opening to insert a baby bottle.

Boudoir Dolls — Mainly decorative and not intended as toys, these come with cloth bodies; exaggerated long limbs; heads of cloth, composition, wax, china, or suede; mohair or silk floss wigs; painted facial features; fashionable costumes; typically unmarked.

Breather Dolls — With pierced or open nostrils.

Brevete — French marking indicating a registered patent.

Bte — Patent registered.

Celebrity Doll — A doll portraying a well-known personality, figure or celebrity; also called a "Personality Doll."

Celluoid — An early, brittle plastic, popular from about 1915 to the 1920s.

Character Doll — Dolls molded to look lifelike; may be infants, children, or adults. Often refers to German bisque dolls produced during the Art Reform Movement of 1909-1925.

Chevrot-style — A doll with wooden lower legs on an articulated kid body, named for Henri Chevrot, who bought the French doll maker Bru Jne & Cie, in 1883.

Child Doll — Typical "dolly-face" dolls.

China — Glazed porcelain.

Cloth Doll — Though sometimes made from patterns, these dolls were also commercially manufactured. Homemade examples are considered folk art.

Composition Body — A harder, more durable version of papier-mâché; also may have included wood pulp, glue, sawdust, flour, or rags.

Crazing — Fine lines that develop on the painted surface of composition.

Crier — a small "voice box" inserted in to the body of dolls, producing a crying or "Mama" sound when they doll is moved.

D.E.P. — A claim to registration.

Dolly-Face — Typical child doll face.

Domed Head — A style of head which has no opening or cut at the top. Common on German dolls of late 19th century; also called "Bald Head."

D.R.G.M. — German marking indicating a registered design.

Eye Chip — Small damage to the rim above or below the eye. Could affect value if large, often ignored when minute.

Eye Mold — Film (usually white) that forms over the eyes of dolls that have been improperly stored or exposed to moisture. May also contribute to rusted interior parts, mildew odor or fabric damage.

Fashion Doll — A doll with a more mature body, narrow waist and bust line and usually has "high heel feet" (see Poupée).

Feathered Brows — Eyebrows painted with many tiny strokes.

Firing Line — In bisque, occurs during the manufacturing process. Seldom affects value.

Five-Piece Body — Body composed of torso, arms, and legs.

Fixed Eyes — Eyes set in a stationary position.

Flange Neck — Doll's neck with ridge and holes at the base for sewing onto a cloth body.

Flirty Eyes — Eyes that move from side to side when head is moved.

Flocked Hair — A coating of short fibers glued to a doll's head to represent hair.

Floss Hair — Embroidery floss used for doll hair, common in the '40s.

Frozen Charlotte — All-porcelain dolls with molded hair and extended arms, sometimes called "German bathing dolls." Designed to float.

Ges (Gesch) — German marking indicating a registered design.

Glass Eyes — Often found in French or German bisque and porcelain dolls made from 1860-1940.

Googly Eyes — Large, round eyes looking to the side.

Gusset — A usually diamond-shaped or triangular insert in a seam to provide expansion or reinforcement.

Gutta-percha — A pinkish-white rubbery, hard, fibrous substance once used to make dolls, bodies, and parts.

Hairline — A line that may or may not be original to the making of a doll, and generally constitutes a faint, thin crack in the bisque.

Half Doll — Dolls molded only from the waist up, sometimes used as toppers for pincushions and handles for brushes; also called pin-cushion dolls.

Hard Plastic — Material used after 1948. Very hard, with excellent impressions and good color.

High-heeled Feet — Feet on fashion dolls that are molded with an arch so they can wear shoes with heels.

Hina-Ningyo — Japanese Festival Doll.

Huminals — Figures having both human and animal characteristics.

Ichimatsu — Japanese play doll.

Immobile — A bisque doll with no joints; molded and cold-painted features and clothing. The cold-painted decoration is usually brightly colored and easily worn. Typically marked "Germany," with a mold number, or unmarked.

Intaglio Eyes — Sunken, rather than cut, eyes that are then painted.

Jointed — A doll that has any number of movable joints.

Karakul — Lamb's skin used to make wigs; sometimes misspelled caracul.

Kid Body — Doll body made of leather.

Lady Doll — Doll with adult face and body proportions.

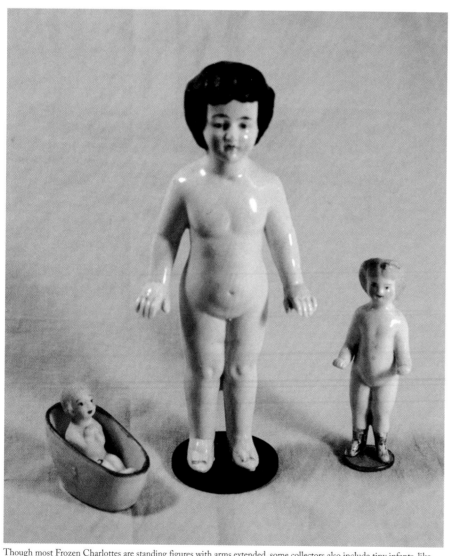

Though most Frozen Charlottes are standing figures with arms extended, some collectors also include tiny infants, like the one seen here in its bath, in this category. The middle doll is about 7" tall. Note the molded shoes on the two standing dolls.

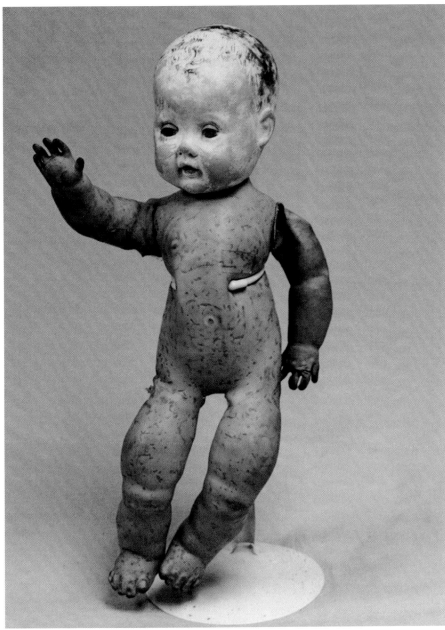

Circa 1950 doll, 13 1/2" tall, with badly deteriorated Magic Skin body and hard-plastic head showing typical white discoloration.

Modern — There is no broad agreement on the proper use of this term. Some apply it to dolls that are less than 25 years old; others use it to describe dolls made since World War II; still others consider all dolls "modern" that were made in the 20th century.

Mohair Wig — Wig made from very fine goat's hair.

Mold Number — Impressed or embossed number that indicates a particular design.

"Motschmann type" — See Taufling; Christopher Motschmann patented a doll voice box in the 1850s.

Multi-Face — A doll whose head can be turned to reveal a different face: sleeping, laughing or crying. The head would be covered by a bonnet or hat, and the faces were changed by spinning a knob on top of the head. Some antique dolls also had multiple heads which could be removed, and which sometimes represented different sexes or races.

Nodders — A bisque doll, solid, one-piece body, joined at the neck by elastic knotted through hole at top of head; stringing enables doll's head to nod; molded and painted features; animal nodders with molded clothes are rare; typically unmarked. Contemporary nodder heads are usually attached with a metal spring.

Open Mouth — Lips parted with opening cut into the bisque. Teeth usually show.

Open/Closed Mouth — Molded mouth appears open, but no opening cut into the bisque.

Original Clothes — Clothes made specifically for the doll at the time it was made, either commercially or homemade.

Painted Bisque — Paint that is not baked into body; brighter in color, but can be rubbed off.

Painted Eyes — Flat, molded, and painted eyes.

Paperweight Eyes — Blown glass eyes with an added crystal to the top resulting in a look with depth and great realism.

Papier-mâché — Material made of paper pulp and glue.

Parian — First used in the mid-19th century, it is a creamy-white, slightly translucent porcelain, deliberately designed to look like the fine marble from the Greek island of Paros, which was used in classical times for important statues.

Pate — Covering for the opening in a doll head. May be made of cardboard, cork, or plaster.

Peppering — Tiny black specks in the slip of many older dolls.

Personality Doll — Dolls molded and fashioned to resemble a famous person.

Look-a-like — Refers to a doll which was produced to look similar to another popular doll of the period (for example, Shirley Temple) and made by another company.

Magic Skin — A rubbery material used for doll skin in the late 1940s and early '50s. They age poorly, becoming dark, deteriorating as the surface turns soft and sticky.

Marks — Imprints of the manufacturer's model or mold numbers on a doll. Often found at the nape of the doll's neck or on its back.

Mask Face — A stiff face that covers only the front of a doll's head.

Matryoshka — Russian nesting doll that opens in the center to reveal a smaller doll. Usually made of wood and painted.

Metal-Head Dolls — First mass-produced in the 1880s, these dolls may consist of all metal or metal head only. Found in aluminum, brass, pewter, silver, steel, tin or other alloys.

MIB — Abbreviation used by collectors to identify dolls that are "mint in the box."

Mint Condition — A doll that is all original, appears to look brand new, and has all its accessories.

These two unmarked German piano babies were intended for a child's instrument, like a Schoenhut piano. The seated figure is about 3" tall.

Piano Babies — Unjointed figures in various positions; with deeply molded and painted hair; painted, often intaglio, eyes; and molded and painted clothes. Reproductions are common.

Pierced Ears — Holes in a doll's ear lobes that go all the way through the lobe.

Pierced-in Ears — Hole for earring passing through doll's ear lobe and straight into doll's head.

Pink Bisque — A later bisque, often early 20th century, which was tinted pink.

Porcelain — A fine grade of clay that is fired at a high temperature. It is translucent in texture and is usually non-porous in the fired state.

Poupée — French term for a fashion doll.

Pouty — Closed mouth doll with a solemn or petulant expression.

Printed Dolls — Doll profiles printed on fabric, which could be cut, sewn and stuffed.

Pug or Pugged Nose — Small, button, slightly turned-up nose.

Queue — Oriental hairstyle of a single plat.

Regional Costume — A traditional costume worn in a specific region or country.

Reproduction — A doll produced from a mold taken from an existing doll.

Rub — A spot where the color has worn away.

Sakura-Ningyo — Traditional Japanese Cherry Doll.

S.F.B.J. — Société Française de Fabrication des Bébés et Jouets, a syndicate formed in 1899 in France to compete with German doll makers.

S.G.D.G. — Registered, but without government guarantee.

Shoulder Head — Head and shoulder in one piece.

Shoulder Plate — Shoulder portion with socket for head.

Snood — A net or fabric bag pinned or tied on at the back of a woman's head for holding the hair; also, a fillet or band for a woman's hair.

Snow Babies — Small unjointed all-bisque figurines, covered with tiny bits of ground porcelain to simulate snow. The best examples were made in Germany in the late 19th and early 20th century. Reproductions are common.

Socket Head — Head with neck that fits into a shoulder plate or the opening of a body.

Solid-dome — Head with no crown opening. May have painted hair or wear a wig.

Stationary Eyes — Glass eyes that do not sleep; also known as staring eyes.

Stockinet — Soft jersey fabric used for dolls.

Straight or Solid Neck — Head is modeled on shoulder plate with no ability to turn or swivel.

Straight Wrists — Hands and arms joined together as one piece with no ball joint or moving part. Sometimes found on an eight-ball-jointed body.

"Taufling type" — From the 1850s, a special body construction, with arms and legs that have "floating" joints, loose and "floppy"; also called a "Motschmann type."

Toddler Body — A short, chubby body of a toddler; often with diagonal joints at hips.

Turned Head — Shoulder head with head slightly turned.

UNIS — An acronym for the Union Nationale Inter-Syndicale, a mark found after 1915 on various French dolls produced by the Société Française de Fabrication des Bébés et Jouets (S. F.B.J.)

Vinyl — A polymer material used after 1950.

Walker Body — Head moves from side to side when legs are made to walk.

Watermelon Mouth — A closed, smiling mouth, usually with a single line.

Wax — An old technique for doll-making; it can be worked in many ways including modeling, carving and casting.

Wax Over — Doll with head and/or limbs (usually of papier-mâché, sometimes composition) covered with a layer of wax to give a lifelike finish.

Weighted Eyes — Sleep eyes that operated by means of a weight attached to a wire frame holding the eyes.

Reproductions

There is almost no area of antique collecting that is not plagued by fakes and reproductions. For collectors of vintage dolls, the only way to avoid reproductions is experience: Making mistakes and learning from them; talking with other collectors and dealers; finding reputable resources (including books and Web sites), and learning to invest wisely, buying the best examples one can afford.

Beginning collectors will soon learn that marks can be deceiving; paper labels and tags are often missing, and those that remain may be spurious.

How does one know whether the numbers incised on a doll's head, or on the limbs at the joints, are authentic? Does a doll look old, and to what degree can patina be simulated? What is the difference between high-quality vintage bisque dolls and modern mass-produced examples? Even experts are fooled when trying to assess qualities that have subtle distinctions.

There is another important factor to consider. A contemporary doll maker may create a "reproduction" doll in tribute of the original, and sell it for what it is: a legitimate copy. Many of these are dated and signed by the artist or manufacturer, and these legitimate copies are highly collectible today. Such dolls are not intended to be frauds.

But a contemporary doll may pass through many hands between the time it leaves the maker and winds up in a collection. When profit is the only motive of a reseller, details about origin, ownership and age can become a slippery slope of guesses, attribution and—unfortunately—fabrication.

As the collector's eye sharpens, and the approach to inspecting and assessing a doll's condition improves, it will become easier to buy with confidence. And a knowledgeable collecting public should be the goal of all sellers, if for no other reason than the willingness to invest in quality.

James D. Julia Inc.
Auctioneers and Appraisers

One of North America's leading auction companies, James D. Julia Inc., was founded in the mid-1960s in Fairfield, Maine.

The firm's specialty divisions include Firearms, Glass and Lamps, Decoys, Antique Advertising, Toys and Dolls, Americana, and Victoriana. Special catalogues, fully illustrated, are offered with most auctions. The descriptions for these offerings are prepared by some of the nation's leading experts.

In the fall of 2003, James D. Julia Inc., sold the doll collection of Mr. and Mrs. Stanwood Schmidt, the results of which are featured in this book. Highlights include:

A 17th century William & Mary wooden doll that sold for $46,000.

A 28" Bèbè Mothereau doll (1880 to 1895) that sold for $15,525.

An 18" Huret child doll (second half of the 19th century) that sold for $13,800.

A 22" Black Simon & Halbig 1358 doll (second half of the 19th century) that sold for $10,350.

An 11" Bruno Schmidt 537 "Wendy" doll (early 20th century) that sold for $7,475.

For more information, contact:
James D. Julia Inc.
P.O. Box 830
Fairfield, ME 04937
Phone: (207) 453-7125
Fax: (207) 453-2502
www.juliaauctions.com
jjulia@juliaauctions.com